SPECIAL EDUCATOR'S DISCIPLINE HANDBOOK

Richard E. Maurer

THE CENTER FOR APPLIED
RESEARCH IN EDUCATION
West Nyack, New York 10995

© 1988 by

THE CENTER FOR APPLIED
RESEARCH IN EDUCATION
West Nyack, NY

All rights reserved.

10 9 8 7 6 5

TO MY PARENTS, TO JEANNETTE AND
REGINA, AND ESPECIALLY TO ELIZABETH

ISBN   0-87628-771-2

THE CENTER FOR APPLIED
RESEARCH IN EDUCATION
BUSINESS & PROFESSIONAL DIVISION
A division of Simon & Schuster
West Nyack, New York 10995

Printed in the United States of America

ABOUT THE AUTHOR

Richard E. Maurer, Ph.D. (Fordham University), has over seventeen years of experience as a classroom teacher, school psychologist, and administrator at every grade level. Currently principal of the Anne M. Dorner Middle School in Ossining, New York, Dr. Maurer has directed a special-education treatment center serving students between the ages of 7 and 21, and has trained teachers from across the country in effective instructional and discipline techniques under Project Intercept (a U.S. Department of Education validated program).

In addition to publishing articles in leading educational and psychological journals and directing workshops at national and regional professional meetings, Dr. Maurer is also the author of *Elementary Discipline Handbook: Solutions for the K-8 Teacher* (The Center for Applied Research in Education, 1985). He has also been appointed to the New York State Education Department's Regents Examination Review Board.

ABOUT THIS HANDBOOK

Special Educator's Discipline Handbook is no ordinary book on school discipline. Unlike most other discipline books, it views the child as a complex individual who has behavior, thoughts, and feelings. At the same time, it views the child in relationship to the community and the family. *Special Educator's Discipline Handbook* treats children as social individuals who need to be nurtured, trained, allowed to mature, and, most important, to be loved as individuals.

It has been written for those special-education teachers looking for innovative, creative, and proven successful classroom management and discipline techniques. You will find hundreds of strategies for dealing with children's behavior, thoughts, feelings, family, and community. In many cases, the strategies are illustrated with actual student, teacher, and/or parent dialogue. In addition, you will find many strategies demonstrated by showing you exactly what to say and how to say it. For example:

- Chapter 1 gives a detailed description of strategies to change student behavior. The goal of these strategies is the immediate change of inappropriate student behavior. You will learn how to establish many types of behavior modification programs, time-out rooms, and student self-control procedures. Six other strategies are also included that will produce immediate results. Those teachers who work with angry students will find numerous procedures and tactics to take control of potentially disruptive incidents and, if the case calls for it, how to defuse explosive student behavior.

- In contrast, Chapter 2 presents behavior change techniques geared to changing the thinking process of students. You will be shown eight different strategies that will guide a student toward creative problem-solving of frustrating situations. Students will be taught how to change the way they think about problems as the first step in changing how they deal with them. After reading this chapter, you will be able to deliver more effective reprimands and deal with student resistance to change. You will also be able to direct students to act more responsibly and to understand why they act out.

- Chapter 3 introduces seven strategies to help you work effectively with parents, because no child is without the influence of family and community. Both of these social structures can be very powerful helpers in assisting a teacher to change student behavior. You will learn how to understand and control the varied pressures and interactions at parent and IEP conferences, back-to-school nights, and other meetings. Procedures to deal with angry parents and group meetings of parents are discussed, and reproducible handouts are included that provide parents with timely advice on child-rearing procedures.

- Chapter 4 is presented as a total curriculum on how to make students feel good about themselves. For each month of the school year, you are given specific student activities spelled out in detail. These activities help improve interpersonal relations, self-esteem, values, social-life skills, listening and communication skills, awareness of group pressure, and mutual support and help. In total, 40 different activities are described for you to use immediately.

- Chapter 5 is devoted to special problems, such as how to deal with emotional crises, student suicide, study problems, and conflictual interpersonal relations. While these problems are shared by a great many young people today, there is a strong feeling among special-education teachers that these problems have a tremendous impact on children with learning problems. Specific ready-to-use strategies are discussed with regard to each of these problems.

Here are steps you may consider when implementing a certain strategy described in this book:

1. *Read.* Read the technique you want to implement and determine what its particular outcome could be in your classroom. Compare and contrast this outcome with possible other outcomes you desire. Once you have decided you want this particular outcome, read the technique again for the specific process or steps involved.

2. *Practice.* Practice the technique either to yourself or in front of a colleague. You may even consider a rehearsal by imagining yourself implementing the different stages of the technique and trying to guess what the outcome will be with different students in the class.

3. *Implement.* Try the technique with a particular student or the entire class. If you are attempting a particular confrontation or discipline technique, first try it out on a student who is not your worst discipline problem. This gives you the opportunity to refine your technique before trying it on the toughest case. Or, you may want to use only part of the technique with a particular student or class. This gives you the opportunity to phase in the technique in different steps. (Most of the procedures described in this handbook can be implemented in such stages.)

4. *Refine.* Refine the technique after your first few attempts by deciding what works and what does not work. Decide if the technique accomplishes your desired outcome. If not, try a different technique and discuss its merits with a colleague.

5. *Implement Again.* Try the technique again. There is no better insurance than to know that you can repeat your performance. You may be surprised at how the implementation process can vary slightly with different types of students but still produce your desired outcome.

A special feature of *Special Educator's Discipline Handbook* are the full-page, ready-to-use forms that can be duplicated as many times as needed for use with students, parents, and other teachers. These forms include "Behavior Rating Chart," "Time-Out Room Report," "A Parent's Guide to Study Tips," "Behavorial Contract," "Personal Stress Chart," and a depression/suicide fact sheet.

As you read this book, you will naturally be comparing some of the strategies to some of the specific children you teach. You will be looking for a technique that will work with a particular student in a given situation. You will also be looking for a good fit based on your own personality and classroom. More than likely, you will need to adapt many of these techniques to meet your needs. I encourage you to do so, because every technique described in *Special Educator's Discipline Handbook* will help you in your classroom.

Richard E. Maurer

CONTENTS

chapter 1

TECHNIQUES FOR CHANGING STUDENT BEHAVIOR

The strategies discussed in this section have as their immediate goal to change student behavior. The common procedure employed with each strategy involves applying behavioral change techniques. After reading this chapter, a teacher will be able to structure the classroom rules and regulations in such a manner that appropriate behavior is increased and inappropriate behavior is easily extinguished.

These strategies do not require that the teacher become involved in the cognitive thinking process of students. *Why* a student behaves in such a manner is not our concern. Rather, we are interested here in the *how*. Specifically, what does this student do and when to cause classroom management problems? The teacher requires no more than a behavioral change from the student. A change in thinking is not a required goal for the strategies in this chapter to work. For example, using the strategies in this chapter, you might want to get Johnny to produce more completed workbook assignments every day. You would not be primarily concerned with the fact that one of the reasons he does not complete the work is that he is bored.

The advantages of the strategies discussed here are that they can be applied easily, show immediate results, and produce enduring change. The disadvantage is that you do not become particularly involved with the feelings or thoughts that motivated the student's behavior.

HOW TO ESTABLISH A BEHAVIOR
MODIFICATION PROGRAM

There are many types of behavior modification programs used in classrooms. As a teacher, you could adopt any of these examples to fit your particular classroom needs. In general, there are two different types of behavior modification programs. One type is directed at the individual student, and the second focuses on all of the students in the room. A few examples are given in this section.

Regardless of how many students you have, the following key elements always need to be incorporated:

- *Decide what behavior you want the student to demonstrate.* Do you want the student to spend more time in his or her seat, to swear less, and to complete more workbook assignments? What specifically do you want to change? You may even want to establish a baseline count of this behavior. For example, you may want to keep count of how many times the student gets out of the seat during class, swears, and completes workbook pages over a particular classroom time.

- *Inform the student.* Be frank and honest with the student. Tell the student that you expect some change in behavior and specify what the change should be. Use your baseline data to support your need to have the student change.

- *Negotiate the reward.* Don't expect the student to change just because you wish so. The student may not have the will or motivation to change. Look for something the student would like to have or do. Is there something you allow in the class that all students consider a privilege? Perhaps this ordinary privilege should now be "earned" with good behavior. There are many types of rewards that could be used. A few examples would be: more recess time, extra praise, early dismissal, stickers, pin, pencil, food, or being permitted to bring items from home. When you negotiate the reward, inform the student that if he or she does _____, then _____ will happen.

- *Start the behavior program.* Be fair and consistent in your counting of behaviors and your dispensing of rewards. In the beginning, there will be times the student will not maintain the desired behavior. Ignore these slight reversals by not saying anything to the student other than he did not earn the reward that day and he will need to try harder.

- *What if you fail?* Check to see if you are asking the student to do too much. If a student is out of her seat a lot during class, it may be more appropriate and easier to ask the student to remain in her seat more rather than to ask her to remain in the seat and complete work. First, work on getting the student to remain in the seat; then work on getting the student to produce. Finally, check the reward. Is it motivating enough, or is it something the student does not care about? A student who is always forgetting a pen may not find receiving a pen an interesting enough reward.

The Desk Chart

For elementary-school students, a teacher may want to use an individual behavior modification technique utilizing a desk chart. Each Monday, a chart similar to the one shown in Figure 1-1 is taped to each student's desk, usually in the upper right-hand corner. Students accumulate "stars" for behavior that the teacher thinks is usually positive for that particular child. The star could be ink-stamped or it could be a glued decal.

Each Monday morning, the teacher informs each child which specific behavior can earn a star. For Rich, it might be not yelling; for Helen, it might be not teasing Ginny; and for Bridie, it might be completing two pages of her math workbook each day.

The reward needs to be negotiated for each child. Look for a high-interest item for the student. On Friday afternoon, set aside the last hour for students to receive their rewards. For some students, buying time to play games, to cook, to paint, to put models together, and even to race batter-powered cars about the school halls are very attractive incentives.

Determining how many "stars" a student needs to accumulate each week to be allowed to spend an hour with his or her reward is an individualized process. As a teacher, you know how much change a student can achieve on a daily basis. Use this knowledge to reward a child.

For example, Anthony usually pulls Regina's hair while in line to go to recess. The teacher decides that this behavior is the one to be targeted for this week. Each time Anthony stands in the recess line and does not pull Regina's hair, he is given a star. The teacher decides that since Anthony has always pulled Regina's hair, asking him to stop for five straight days would be asking for a miracle. Rather than frustrating Anthony totally and allowing the behavior modification program to fail, the teacher asks Anthony to stop for three days out of five. Anthony perceives this request as reasonable. Figure 1-2 shows Anthony's desk chart for the week.

Anthony achieved his goal and received the reward. It was a difficult task for him, and he needed to be praised and reminded each day of how he was doing.

Mon.	Tues.	Wed.	Thurs.	Fri.
★ ★	★	★	★ ★ ★	★

Figure 1–1

Mon.	Tues.	Wed.	Thurs.	Fri.
★		★	★	

Figure 1–2

The next week, the teacher asked Anthony for four days of not pulling Regina's hair. By the third week, Anthony was required not to pull the girl's hair for five days.

The Class Store

This behavior modification technique is very appropriate for a self-contained class structure. Students can earn daily points for displaying appropriate behavior. These points are accumulated over a period of weeks and can be used like money to "purchase" items from the class store. The store itself is usually a large trunk or wooden box containing various high-interest items priced at different costs. The store is open for business every Friday afternoon for a period of an hour. During this time, students can view the items in the store and decide either to "purchase" an item or to save their points to use toward a future purchase. Some students just like to accumulate points and decide *never* to "purchase" an item. (See Figure 1-3.)

Two student "accountants" check the books the day following the store opening and make sure that the adding and subtracting of points by the store cashiers is correct. On the same day, these students distribute slips of paper to each student reporting the amount of points remaining in each account.

A teacher may ask parents at the beginning of the school year for items from the home. Typical tag-sale items that have a high student interest are appropriate. The school principal may also contribute items from the school supply list. Typical items in the class store are:

Student	Savings (Points)	Item	Cost	Present Accumulation (Points)
Mary	105	Pen	50	55
Joe	50	Pencil	1	49

Figure 1_3

pencils　　　　　　paper　　　　　　games
pens　　　　　　　junk jewelry　　　food items
note pads　　　　　old clothing

The Class Chart

This technique combines the influence of peer pressure with that of individual behavior modification. Students earn points daily for demonstrating positive behavior. These points are recorded daily on a "Behavior Rating Chart" posted in the classroom. At the end of the week, those students who have accumulated a predetermined level of points will be rewarded. On Monday, the teacher and students start over again with a new "Behavior Rating Form" and a new predetermined level of points.

This technique is particularly suited for a self-contained class or a resource-room setting. The teacher, for example, may establish 40 points as the number to achieve by Friday afternoon. A sample rating chart is shown in Figure 1-4. Form 1-1 is a blank "Behavior Rating Chart" that can be copied for immediate use.

Each day, the teacher awards points to the students and keeps a log on the desk. At the end of the day and before the whole class, the teacher shades in or colors in the total amount of points a student received that day. In our example, Lynn has accumulated 4 points, Regina 6, Tom 4, and James 5.

The reward given at the end of the week could be anything that contains a high-interest level. Commonly used are food items from the school cafeteria. A teacher may arrange to open an account with the cafeteria manager for this purpose. Some principals will establish a purchase order of a set amount ($70, for example) with the cafeteria company from which the special education teacher can draw. On Friday, those students who accumulated the predetermined amount of

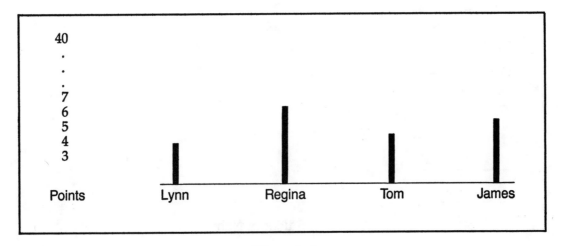

Figure 1–4

BEHAVIOR RATING CHART

Points	Student's Names
_____	
_____	
_____	
_____	
_____	
_____	
_____	
_____	
_____	
_____	
_____	
_____	
_____	
_____	
_____	
_____	
_____	
_____	
_____	
_____	
_____	

Form 1-1

points would be given a credit slip entitling that person to a free package of cookies, french fries, an apple, or a cup of juice.

A strong motivator of change that is built into this technique is peer pressure. With the public posting of a "Behavior Rating Chart," every student in the class can see and be aware of how everyone else is doing. Students often will try to be the first to achieve the predetermined point level and will try not to be the one with the lowest point level.

As for establishing the point level needed to achieve a reward, the teacher should make the level high enough that most students need to work until Friday to make it. If a student makes the predetermined level by Wednesday and the reward is assured, there is the danger that the student would just stop displaying such positive behavior until the following Monday. Another factor to consider is that the predetermined reward level can be adjusted up or down every week depending on how many students can or cannot make it. Ideally, it would be nice if every student made the reward level on Friday. This would reveal a positive determination by each student to achieve positive behavior. Most likely, however, there will be a few students who do not make it. This is appropriate, for the fact that so many of their peers made it may serve as a motivation to these students. What is nice about the weekly charting is that each student has the opportunity to start fresh. A student having a bad week is not penalized for doing poorly when he or she begins a new week in school.

HOW TO ESTABLISH A TIME-OUT ROOM THAT WORKS

Frequently used by teachers, *time-out* is a successful technique aimed at a variety of different student populations. There is no one definition of time-out used in the literature, because the technique has such broad uses. For our purposes, there are three different types of time-out procedures:

- *Isolation.* The student is removed from a classroom to a place where there is very little to do and no one to speak with.
- *Partial exclusion.* The student is placed in a part of the classroom where he or she cannot view the class or participate in its activities.
- *Total exclusion.* The student is sent to a supervised room removed from the classroom where he or she is required to complete classroom work assignments.

The chief advantage of the time-out procedure is that it removes a student who is disruptive or fails to work from a teacher's attention, even though it may be for a short time. The teacher is free to devote his or her energy and time to promote the learning environment for the remainder of the students. A second advantage is that there is some positive change in behavior—even for only a while—while the student is involved in the time-out procedure.

The disadvantage of this procedure is that students view time-out as a punishment. It is evident in the research that punishment is the least powerful tool in changing a student's behavior. Therefore, if the teacher desires to change student behavior over a sustained period, the time-out procedure should not be the only technique used. Coupled with other techniques described in Chapters 1 and 2, however, time-out is an excellent beginning. If nothing else, the teacher's use of such a technique informs the student that his or her behavior has gone beyond the limit of acceptability.

Isolation

In a school setting, it is never appropriate to place a child alone in a locked room. If a child is so disruptive that removal from a room is necessary, it is important that the child be accompanied by an adult. If the child is to be placed in another room, the adult should accompany the child into the room. If the child continues to be disruptive in the isolation room, the teacher should implement the techniques recommended to deal with angry students that are described at the end of this chapter.

As with any time-out procedure, it is best first to warn the child that his or her behavior is inappropriate and that, if it continues, he or she will be placed in the time-out room. Second, keep the child in an isolation time-out room for only a short period of time. As the child calms down, the teacher should move him or her to a different type of time-out room, such as total exclusion. From there, as the student becomes more socially attuned, he or she can be moved to partial exclusion time-out and eventually back to the full participation with the other students in the class.

The following is an example of isolation used with a seven-year-old girl, Laura, who is classified as an ED student. Laura had a temper tantrum during class. The teacher requested that the classroom aide cover the class while she accompanied Laura to the time-out room.

The teacher took Laura to a classroom which was completely empty of books, desks, and tables. Laura was asked to sit in a chair and told to relax. The teacher sat on the other side of the room. The dialogue that ensued is recorded below:

TEACHER: Now, Laura, just relax. I would like you to just sit there and relax. I'll sit here, and when you want to talk, just tell me.

LAURA: [Sits, but just continues to weep.]

TEACHER: Just relax now, Laura. It will be all right.
[The teacher realizes that Laura needs time to calm down and to collect herself.]
When you are ready to talk, please tell me. I would like to listen—to hear your view.

LAURA: [Has stopped weeping, but continues to stare blankly ahead.]

TEACHER: You know, Laura, calming down the way you have is not easy. I am proud of you. When you want to talk about it, just raise your hand to signal me.

LAURA: [Raises her hand after a few minutes.]

TEACHER: [Moves closer to Laura and begins to discuss with her the causes of her temper tantrum. When she feels that Laura is ready to go back to class, she escorts her.]

Partial Exclusion

Most classrooms have an area in which a single desk or chair that does not have direct visual access to the other desks can be placed. A time-out room of this nature is usually established behind a file cabinet, wall divider, or coat closet. The most appropriate type of student to place in this area is one whose disruptive behavior is not severe enough nor dangerous enough that the student needs to be physically separated from the other students. Neither the teacher nor aide need sit with the student, who should be visible.

It is assumed that a student placed in partial time-out has sufficient composure to maintain self-control. Therefore, it is appropriate to give the child some classwork to be completed while in time-out. The work should be review work, not work that requires the teacher to answer questions. Alternatively, the student can fill out a questionnaire (see Form 1-2) explaining why he or she was placed into the time-out area and outlining what the student will be doing to change his or her behavior. Typical questions would be as follows:

1. What did I do to get in here?
2. How did this behavior help me?
3. How can I get out?
4. What will I do to change?

The completed questionnaire serves as an excellent counseling instrument for the teacher to use with the student.

There are a variety of forms of partial time-out, a few of which are listed below:

1. *Out-the-door.* The student must stand outside the classroom door until the teacher asks him or her to return. For younger children, this time should be kept short. Hallways are very public, and younger children can be frightened if left there too long. For older children, the time can be extended to include the entire class period, if necessary. However, if the hallways in your school are very busy, leaving a child in the hall might lead to inappropriate socializing and other disruptions. It is best to tell the student to stand up and to

Name_____ Date_____

TIME-OUT ROOM REPORT

Please answer all questions. If you need more space to write, use the
back of this sheet.

1. What did I do to get in here? _____

_____

_____

_____

_____

2. How did this behavior help me? _____

_____

_____

_____

_____

3. How can I get out? _____

_____

_____

_____

_____

4. What will I do to change? _____

_____

_____

_____

_____

Form 1-2

write something. It is best that the writing be meaningful, not just a task of writing one hundred times, "I must obey the teacher." Such tasks are seen as meaningless and often as punishing by the children. If you would like to make the time-out meaningful, have the student write something related to the academic lesson that he or she is missing or fill in the questionnaire discussed earlier.

2. *Stay-for-lunch.* Some teachers require students to stay inside during lunch time. This form of time-out often is used to make the student complete work missed. The student is deprived of socializing during lunch, but is required to complete work instead. This often is seen as a punishment by students, but some students view it as a special opportunity to talk to the teacher. Staying with the teacher and eating with the teacher can be rewarding enough to some that they disrupt the class purposefully to attain this reinforcement. One should always be watchful for cases such as these.

3. *Taking-off-the-ribbon.* This procedure is especially popular with younger children. Here the teacher distributes ribbons, buttons, and medals to all the children at the start of class. If a student becomes very disruptive, he or she is asked to remove the ribbon, button, or medal. During this time, the teacher must not offer attention nor allow the child the opportunity to participate in classroom activities. This procedure should be implemented only for a short time after the disruptive behavior has ceased (two to three minutes). What is unique about this procedure is that all the children are rewarded for just coming to class and participating.

Total Exclusion (Time-Out Room)

With this type of time-out, the student is removed from the classroom. Unlike isolation, however, the student is not kept from interacting with others. Probably the most popular form of time-out is sending a student to the principal's office. While there is the immediate gain for the teacher in that the child has been removed from class, going to the school's main office often is seen by the student as a positive step. He or she receives extra attention form secretaries, often helps out in the office, and has the opportunity to socialize with all who enter the office.

A more appropriate total exclusion time-out procedure is the use of a school-wide time-out room. Such a room, described below, could be manned by teachers during duty periods or by school aides. Open all day long, such a room is a very efficient manner for school administrators and counselors to deal with students who may be having problems learning that day.

GOAL OF A TIME-OUT ROOM.   The time-out room has one goal—to provide a resource for the teachers in the building. Any staff member may send a student to the time-out room at any time during the day. The room will allow teachers to be freed of disruptive students so that the other students in the classroom are not deprived of learning time. The room of itself cannot change the student's disruptive behavior. Other school resources, such as counselors, psychologists, or parent conferences, will be required to meet this need.

OPERATING THE TIME-OUT ROOM.   When a teacher sends a student to the time-out room, a disciplinary referral form must accompany the student. (See Form 1-3.) On the form, the student's behavior should be classified as A, B, or C. These codes (described below) will alert the principal as to the appropriate action. If no classification is indicated, the disruption should be considered an A. Students referred should be disruptive enough to warrant removal from class. The teacher and the administrator will need to work to improve the student's behavior. The room should not be a dumping ground for students.

CLASSIFICATION OF STUDENT'S BEHAVIOR.   There are three behavior classifications:

1.   *Type A:* The student will only be excluded from class for the class period. At the end of the period, the student may return to class. Reasons for this referral might be refusal to work, disturbing others, excessive noise, or refusing to follow directions. The staff member making the referral will follow up with a parent phone call.

2.   *Type B:* The student will be excluded from class until the appropriate assistant principal or dean sees the student. This classification is reserved for disruptive behaviors that are chronic in nature. For example, a student who is late to class four days in a row could receive this classification. The administrator will contact the teacher with regard to the status of the action.

3.   *Type C:* The student will be excluded from class until the principal sees the student. Usually, this classification is reserved for the most serious offenses such as fighting, verbal abuse to a teacher, smoking, etc.

It is suggested that at the end of the school day a list of all students placed in the time-out room be typed and distributed to teachers. This information will be helpful to teachers who sent children to the time-out room to make sure they arrived, to the other teachers in the building who teach the child, and to others who might question why a child missed a class period when records indicate the student attended school.

Form 1-3, "School Discipline Referral," can be kept in a book in the time-out room. Information from the individual referral slips can then be collated by the teacher on duty. If your school has access to a personal computer, it is very easy to set up a filing and report system to keep track of which students were sent to the time-out room and how often. Any file form could be used; Form 1-4 is one example.

SCHOOL DISCIPLINE REFERRAL

Name of Student_____ Time_____

Description of Incident: _____

_____

_____

_____

Incident Classifications: A   B   C

_____
Teacher   Date

Form 1-3

INDIVIDUAL RECORD OF REFERRALS

Name of Student_____ Grade_____

Number of Referrals: _____

Dates: _____

_____

Number of Classifications: A _____

B _____

C _____

Form 1-4

HOW TO TEACH STUDENTS TO CONTROL THEIR OWN BEHAVIOR

The opportunity to teach students how to control their own behavior is a teacher's dream come true. The process of how to go about this is relatively easy to implement, and the success rate is very high. The primary positive feature of this procedure is its efficiency—the student does most of the work! The student self-observes, self-records, self-evaluates, and can even determine his or her own rewards. The teacher is freed from maintaining an external behavioral control system. This technique is particularly useful for a student who has some motivation to change but does not know how to go about it or lacks the will power. This technique is not recommended as the primary change procedure for a student who lacks the motivation to change. There are six key steps to implement this technique.

Determine a Behavior

Decide which behavior of the student you would like to change. Make sure the behavior is concrete and specific and can be observed. For example, behaviors listed below fit this criteria:

- Sitting in the seat
- Not swearing
- Coming prepared
- Not throwing paper
- Completing two homework assignments

Behaviors such as those listed below are less able to be observed and recalled, because they are so general and are based on subjective opinion:

- Behaving properly
- Completing work
- Leaving others alone
- Not wandering around

The best way to pick a behavior to change is to observe a student for a period of time and list those things which he or she does that annoy you. In a 15-minute period for example, a teacher recorded a 10-year old EMR student named Art doing the following:

- Throws paper
- Makes gutteral sounds
- Jumps up and down from his desk

In this case, the teacher picked one of these behaviors as annoying her the most. The one chosen was "jumps up and down from his desk."

Observe and Record

For the next three days, you will need to be patient and try not to change anything. Just observe this behavior, and record how often it appears.

Once you have some record of the behavior over a period of time, you will be able to judge how severe the problem is and will have a basis to determine in the future if there has been some change in behavior.

In our example, the teacher recorded the following behavior for Art. During a particular class period of 42 minutes, the teacher divided the period into four 10-minute sections. She set the timer (regular kitchen-type) at the beginning of each 10-minute period. She then recorded whether Art got out of his seat without permission or not during this 10-minute interval. She did not count the number of times—rather just whether the behavior occurred or not. On a record sheet, she recorded either a Y (for yes) or a N (for no) over a three-day period. Figure 1-5 shows the record sheet she constructed. You can see from this record sheet that Art is out of his seat without permission for much of the class period.

Intervene

The student will need to be introduced to your behavior control plan. The best way to accomplish this is by being straight-forward and honest. Here is a dialogue between Art and his teacher:

> TEACHER: Listen, Art, when you get out of your seat so often during class, you disrupt me and the others. I am annoyed and upset by this and would like you to change. Art, you need to change and spend more time in your seat. I have a plan to help you, but I need your help.
>
> ART: I do not get out of my seat that much. Jerry, he is the one.
>
> TEACHER: How about finding out yourself? You count whether you get out of your seat or not, and I will count also. Let's compare at the end of class.
>
> ART: OK, let's try.

Figure 1–5

Minute Internal		Day 1	Day 2	Day 3
40		Y	Y	Y
30		N	Y	Y
20		Y	N	Y
10		Y	Y	N

Days

Self-Record

At this time, the teacher should show the student the record sheet she has kept for the past three days. She should explain how she made the sheet and how she put the marks on it. The student should be given a blank record sheet and be allowed to practice filling it in. Depending on the age of the student, a few practice sessions or attempts will be needed. Make sure the student knows exactly how to record the behavior in question. You may find that some adjustments in how the record sheet is designed will be needed to make the student's task as simple as possible.

At the next class, hand the student a record sheet, set the timer (if you are using one), and tell the student to record as practiced. For the first few times, it is helpful to keep a record for yourself. In our example, Art completed Figure 1-6, while the teacher completed Figure 1-7.

The key to implementing this self-control process is in designing the self-recording sheet the student will be using. The sheet must be simple enough for the student to understand, but comprehensive enough to record the information on the behavior as you want it. If you are caught in a conflict between these two criteria, always choose the simpler option first. You also need to remember to praise the student when there is evidence that the self-control process is working. Genuine praise goes a long way toward making this process work efficiently and quickly. This technique has been used with first- and second-graders so it has a built-in flexibility provided that the teacher can pinpoint the behavior to be reduced, design a record sheet to record it, and teach the student how to exert self-control.

Compare

It is not important that the teacher's and the student's record of observations show identical results. A discussion of the similarities and contrasts is important, because the process will train the student to be more accurate in self-recording. Try recording a few more times together to see if you and the student can reduce the range of contrasts. Interestingly, discussions with a student about the record of a certain behavior is much less threatening to the student than discussions of the student's behavior itself. There is something more objective about relying on a record sheet when discussing behavior.

Reward or Not?

It is not necessary to give a tangible reward to the student for achieving a reduction of behavior through use of the self-recording process. Often, simple praise is

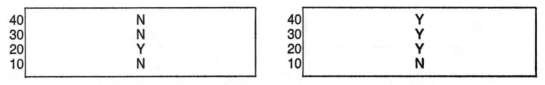

Figure 1–6   Figure 1–7

reward enough. If, however, a teacher decides to give a reward to the student for reducing the behavior for the day, the following criteria should be considered. The major question is whether the student or the teacher should select the reward. You will need to be the judge here. A few guidelines to consider are the following ones: (1) student-selected rewards can be a more powerful factor in behavior change than a teacher's determination of the rewards; (2) some students will choose lenient criteria to receive the reward; (3) with some guidelines and restrictions from a teacher, most students can determine their own reward system; (4) punishing students for not maintaining a certain behavior is not as effective as rewarding a student for maintaining a behavior. In our case with Art, the teacher decided that verbal praise at the end of the class period was a sufficient reward.

The Program

Once you have a sense the student understands how to record his or her own behavior and you have determined whether there will be a reward, begin the behavioral change program. At the beginning of each class period, hand the student the record sheet to be recorded. If you use individualized folders for academic work, you could insert a daily behavior record sheet into it. Set the timer if you are using an external time counter. Rather than embarrass the student when the timer goes off, you might just tell the other students that you are keeping track of time. They need not know that a student is self-recording behavior. Make sure you reset the timer. At the end of the class period, observe the student's record sheet. Be sure to praise the student for any modest gain at reducing the targeted behavior. If the behavior to be eliminated increases, ask the student what went wrong. Do not punish or criticize the student. Simply say that tomorrow will be another day to try. Allow the student to take the record sheet for a file he or she is keeping. On occasion, you may want to use a record sheet yourself to record the student's behavior. By comparing your record and the student's, you can judge whether the student's accountability is on target.

The Outcome

Self-recording can be a treatment unto itself. The change in behavior usually occurs with the student just recording his or her behavior. There is something in just observing one's own actions that produces change. The time it takes to reduce the targeted annoying behavior varies from student to student. Also, the particular behavior being targeted has an effect on the time. As a general rule, however, if you are having a student self-record every class day, you should see some positive movement by the tenth school day. If nothing is happening by this time, you should adopt one of the external behavioral change techniques described later in this chapter.

The overall reduction is usually gradual, and the teacher needs to be patient with the process. Occasional reverses can be expected. There will be days when the student behaves as on the first days of the intervention, which may lead you to question the validity of the self-recording process. Usually, however, these reversals are brief, and the recovery to the reduction level is quick.

In our example with Art, there was a total reduction in out-of-seat behavior within 15 school days. However, there was in immediate decline to only one out-of-seat behavior within five school days. The record sheets Art kept in his file noted this reduction.

Some question always arises about when should the teacher withdraw the self-record process. It is best not to withdraw it too soon, or the targeted behavior may return. It is a good idea to keep the process going for two weeks after the behavior has been totally eliminated. If the behavior returns after you stop the self-record process, it is appropriate to initiate the self-record process again. This time, however, keep the process for at least a month following its elimination.

You will also see a reduction in the annoying behavior of other students in the class. By reducing the disruption of one student, you eliminate the stimulus or influence of distraction on others.

Form 1-5, "Control Sheet," can be used to take notes on the problems and successes you have with an individual student as you implement each of the preceding steps. Keep a control sheet on each student with whom you use the technique.

HOW TO USE PHOTOGRAPHS TO TEACH APPROPRIATE BEHAVIOR

Photographs are a form of nonverbal communication. Students can learn by observing photos. They do not need to verbalize their thoughts nor communicate with another verbally to learn when using this medium. This nonverbal communication is a very powerful means to teach. For students who have problems verbalizing thoughts and feelings, using photographs is one very effective way to teach compliance with rules and regulations.

In addition, a teacher can integrate the science curriculum into this unit if they wish. In schools where photography darkrooms are available, the teacher can have the students develop and print their own photographs. Concepts, such as chemical compounds, physics of light, properties of matter, as well as counting, charting, measuring, and timing skills, can be emphasized. This strategy can be very exciting and meaningful for students.

The strategy itself is divided into six steps. Each is described here in some detail. However, you may want to develop your own modifications as you work through the process.

Method

STEP 1: SELECTION OF RULES AND REGULATIONS.   In many schools, a student handbook is made available to students in which certain rules and regulations of the school are defined. Unfortunately, these handbooks disappear the first

Student's Name _____

CONTROL SHEET

1. Determine a Behavior _____

   _____

   _____

2. Observe and Record _____

   _____

   _____

3. Intervene _____

   _____

   _____

4. Self-record _____

   _____

   _____

5. Compare _____

   _____

   _____

6. Reward or Not? _____

   _____

   _____

7. The Program _____

   _____

   _____

8. The Outcome _____

   _____

   _____

Other Notes:

Form 1-5

month of school in many school buildings. Rules are forgotten unless they are enforced and unless students are reminded of them. For many students, simply stating a rule is not enough. They do not know *how* to comply with the rule. For example, informing a retarded child that he or she must walk up the staircase on the right side of the stairs is not enough. Either the student is taken out of the room and shown how to walk up the stairs or the student is show pictures of how to complete the task in order to reinforce the procedure. There are probably many rules and regulations special education students have difficulty understanding.

In this step, ask the students which of the rules and regulations they do not understand. Pick a few of the rules you feel need special emphasis. Also you may decide that there are other social skills the students lack that need to be emphasized. The age and maturation of the child will determine how much student input you will allow. Perhaps, how to maintain direct body focus when talking and listening, how to stand and wait in the cafeteria line, how to sit at one's desk, how to organize one's desk and locker, and how to shake hands are skills that need reinforcing. The photo technique described here will help you with this process.

At this point, make a list of about ten rules or skills on which you want to focus. Inform the students what you are doing. Tell them you will help them learn how to follow these rules and do these skills with the use of photos. Remind them that they will have fun doing this.

STEP 2: DISCUSSION OF RULES   Hold a number of group discussions with the students to emphasize the rules or skills you have chosen. A lead question may be:

"What would you see if a student was obeying this rule?" Focus the discussion around what students would actually be doing if they were following the rule.

Ask students to observe others in the building following a particular rule or performing a skill you are emphasizing. Ask them to remember or list important points to bring to the next group discussion.

Another procedure is to have the students draw stick-body cartoons of students obeying a rule or following a skill. These drawings can be put on large posterboard for special emphasis.

At this point, help the students summarize their observed information and facts from the group discussion. You could develop a list of behaviors that one could conceivably see when a student was following a rule or performing a skill. Here is such an example to demonstrate the rule that students must walk in a certain manner in the hall and on the stairs when changing classes:

- Walk against the wall
- Do not run
- Hold stair railings
- Stay to the right on the stairs

STEP 3: PHOTO-TAKING SESSION.   This step is the most fun for students. Tell them that they must photograph pictures of students following rules or performing the skills the class has decided to emphasize. Basically, students need to find other students doing the behavior they listed for each rule in Step 2. Students may need to go on "scouting" missions in the school to find "photo" opportunity sessions and/or places.

Selection of cameras and film will depend on your school's inventory. The instant camera is the easiest to use, and the photos can be easily mounted. However, if you are interested in integrating science into this strategy, the use of roll film and the subsequent darkroom activities will be needed. If you have no access to cameras, ask students to bring them in from home. You should be able to locate or borrow enough cameras for every student in the class.

If students cannot find sufficient examples for picture taking, ask them to pose for the pictures among themselves. For shy students, this might be a less threatening alternative than to have them ask students in the building if they could take their pictures.

You may need to give your picture takers a few simple instructions before they venture out into the school looking for photo opportunities. For instance, students may need to ask students to pose, to smile, to stand still, and—most important—to give their permission to be photographed. You may need to have a few practice sessions on how to take good pictures. For younger children, you will need to accompany them. However, let them do the work. The pictures need not be perfect.

STEP 4: PHOTO SELECTION.   Once you have accumulated a sufficient number of photos for each of the rules or skills the students are working on, you need to select the ones which best represent the idea.

Hold group discussions again about the rules of skills on which you are working. Ask students to look at each of the photos and determine which ones best demonstrate the behaviors that were listed in Step 2. It is important that at least one of the photographs that each student has taken be represented so as not to offend anyone.

STEP 5: MOUNTING   You will need to mount the photos. It is suggested that the photos be grouped according to behavior and skill. You may even want to place them in a sequence to shown a "how-to-do" phase. For example, how to go to the cafeteria, pick a tray, select food, and go to the cashier are phases which can be shown in a photo sequence.

Your mounting should be secure enough to keep the photos from curling and falling off the mounting or posterboard. Use a secure glue, not tape. Label everything so the pictures can be understood. For an added touch, students may want to sign the corner of the poster mounting to show their involvement in all the work.

STEP 6: PRESENTATION.   The final step is to have the students present the posters before the class. Here they describe in what way the particular pictures illustrate how to follow a rule or perform a skill. Students or groups who worked on particular photos may want to present their own. Students usually show a lot of pride in their work, so these presentations are very important. Invite interested school officials to the presentation; the principal will be delighted to hear these presentations! Finally, choose an appropriate place in the classroom to display the finished products.

Summary

This strategy takes time to complete. It can be fun, exciting, and personally rewarding to students. Each step in this process involves students discussing, discovering, analyzing, demonstrating, and displaying how to follow rules and how to perform certain skills. The constant repetition reinforces the rules and rewards the students as well for compliance.

HOW TO TEACH STUDENTS TO STOP THEIR OWN INTRUSIVE, HARMFUL THOUGHTS

Many students are troubled with unwanted thoughts that flood their consciousness. Like daydreaming carried to an extreme, compulsive thought-flooding intrudes on one's ability to think clearly, feel relaxed, and even finish a task. These intrusive thoughts become harmful when they lead to unproductivity, arouse anxiety, inhibit behavior, or—even worse—stimulate a series of unwanted behaviors.

There are generally two types of intrusive thoughts. The first only comes to consciousness when the student has finished a task and is switching to another, or when the student takes a break. Thoughts of this type are the weaker of the two, because they usually can be suppressed by having the student engage in a task or interact with a classmate. By such means, these thoughts are kept blocked from intruding for a while.

An example of this type of intrusive thought can be seen with 10-year-old Laurie. Laurie is not bothered with the visual memory of her father hitting her mother last week as long as she is occupied on-task in the class. However, every time Laurie goes to the bathroom or has a moment to relax, the visual image of the fight floods into her consciousness. She has felt sick to her stomach, has thrown up, and has come back to the class late and with a severe headache.

The second type of intrusive thought is much more harmful, because it cannot be kept out of consciousness by suppressing them with other preoccupations. These thoughts are so painful, vivid and arousing that they can surface at any time. Students have trouble sleeping, because these intruding thoughts can even come in dreams and are so intense that the students are awakened.

Peter is a six-year-old EMR student who is troubled with a memory of a dog biting his leg. This event happened over three years ago, but Peter is still troubled with the thought. During story time, animal characters will arouse this thought. The sight of an angry dog will bring on the thought. Peter cannot control the thought. He appears to the teacher to be daydreaming except that he has a frightened look on his face, complains of physical problems, and on occasion starts to cry.

A Twelve-Step Procedure

For a student to reveal troubling thoughts to the teacher may take time. But as the trust and the level of relationship deepens, many students do confide their troubled thoughts. Once this happens, the teacher has an invitation to help the student cope. Follow these steps:

1. Ask the student to list any thoughts which are out of control or which he or she feels are always coming back. Rephrase the statement for the student so that it is in a concrete form. In our example of Laurie, you might say:

    "I'm troubled with the memory of my father hitting my mother with his hand."

    "I'm troubled with the memory of my mother crying and running into the bedroom."

2. Once you have some specific statements to focus on, have a short discussion with the student about how harmful these thoughts can be if they are allowed to continue to come back.

    You might say: "These thoughts do not help you feel better. They do not change what happened and they do not help your father or mother. These thoughts do interfere with your classwork, and they cause you headaches."

3. Outline the process you plan to use to help the student eliminate the harmful thoughts. Refer to the process as "thought-stopping."

4. Prepare the student to relax. Have the student sit in a quiet room and close his or her eyes. Ask the student to take some deep breaths and relax hands, arms, shoulders, chest, stomach, buttocks, legs, knees, ankles, and feet muscles. You may need to repeat the relaxation command. Ask the student to feel the relaxation of muscles and to continue to breathe deeply.

5. Inform the student that he or she is to remember the intrusive thought when you say, "Go." Repeat the specific statement of the thought agreed upon in Step 1. Ask the student to raise his or her finger to signal when the thought or memory begins.

6. Ask the student to relax, breathe deeply, and then say, "Go."

7. When the student raises his or her finger, you should shout out the word, "Stop." The student will be surprised and even startled. Ask the student how he or she feels and whether the thought went away. (It almost always does.)

8. Repeat the procedure a second time, but this time allow the student a few seconds after the finger signal to experience the thought more deeply. Then shout, "Stop." Once again, discuss with the student how he or she feels and whether the thought went away.

9. After these two sessions, inform the student that you are going to teach the technique of thought-stopping so that it can be done anywhere and any place. Ask the student to close his or her eyes and to imagine calling out the word, "Stop." Tell the student to practice this until the "stop" command is clear and strong. Yelling the command "stop" may help the student set the image. For a younger grade-student, a sign saying "stop" would help serve as a reminder.

10. Ask the student to repeat the word "stop" anytime the intrusive thought comes back to consciousness. Also, the student needs to practice saying "stop" at least five times a day for a week.

11. For the student to use this technique with facility, provide sufficient practice until the student reports it works. Usually two sessions, such as that described here, every day for five days should be sufficient to make the student independent.

12. Remind the student that the thought will go away gradually. Parts of the memory will fade sooner than others, but eventually the stop imagery will eliminate it all. During the process, spend time talking to the student about aspects of the thought. In Laurie's case, it is clear that she needs to talk about the events at home that are causing so much stress.

Variation of the Procedure

Rather than "thought stopping," another approach is to apply "thought-switching." In this procedure, a student replaces a negative thought with a positive one. In Peter's case, his thought about "being afraid of dogs" could be switched to "dogs are afraid of Peter." This thought-switching is just a matter of telling the student to "switch" rather than "stop" the thought. Follow the procedure described above with the one change.

HOW TO ELIMINATE A STUDENT'S IRRATIONAL FEARS

For many teachers, one way of defining an irrational fear is as a phobia. Like adults, students have phobias to a greater or lesser degree. Like an adult phobia, a child's phobia may cause social limitations, poor performance, and even bizarre behaviors. Take the case of Joe, an 11-year-old boy who cannot sit at a cafeteria table with other students to eat lunch. Joe eats standing up next to an unoccupied lunch table. He is afraid to sit down, because someone might join him. He is afraid.

The procedure to help a student eliminate irrational fears of this nature is very simple. The essence of the process is to have the student experience the fear or anxiety while in a relaxed behavioral state. Though the combination of relaxation and a progressive re-creation of the fear, the student learns how to cope with the anxiety over time. The desensitization procedure can be done through imagery re-creation by actually having the student participate in the situation or through a group participation. All three examples will be illustrated here.

The Causes of Irrational Fears

The cause of most unwanted fears is usually fear of feelings rather than fear of animals, high places, lunch rooms, being touched, closed rooms, etc. Student fears of their own feelings (interim fears) get translated into an elaborate phobia or fear of something (external fears). Rather than deal with the fear inside themselves, students will create an impressive fear outside themselves. Depending on psychological orientation, some teachers will intervene with the fears inside the student, while others will just intervene with the symptoms of these fears—the fears outside. In our example, Joe has created an obsessional/compulsive fear of the school cafeteria to mask his own fear of being rejected by others.

Figure 1-8 illustrates how these fears inside Joe become cloaked with fears outside of himself.

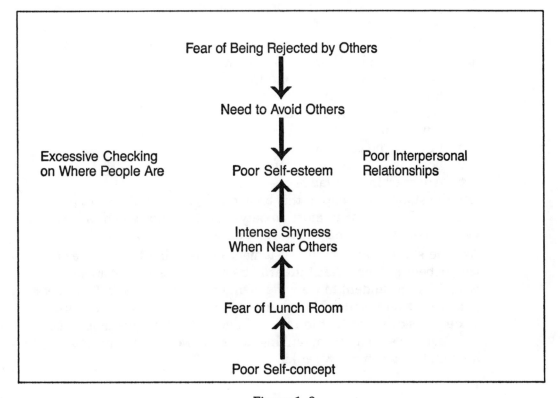

Figure 1–8

Starting from the top in the figure, you have Joe's external fear; starting from the bottom, you have Joe's internal fear. The common meeting point or shared cause is Joe's poor self-esteem.

A 7-Step Procedure

The purpose of this technique is to treat the symptoms. When applied systematically, the technique will gradually help Joe to begin to sit down at a lunchroom cafeteria table and eat with others. The technique may or may not help Joe with his internal fear of being rejected, but it will produce a specific behavioral change. (For the teacher interested in attacking the internal fear, it is suggested that techniques described in Chapter 4, "Strategies to Improve Student Feelings About Themselves," be implemented.)

1. Ask the student to help construct a personal anxiety scale. First, ask the student for the one event or thing he or she can remember that caused the most anxiety or fear. Give this event a rank of 100. Then ask the student for the one event or thing he or she can remember that causes the most feelings of calm or relaxation. Rank this a 0 level. Then ask for an event that can be ranked at the 50th level, or half way between total fear and total relaxation.

2. Teach the student to relax by using the muscle relaxation method described in Figure 1-9. This method should also be used at home every night by the student.

3. Take a student fear—in our case we will use Joe's fear of the lunchroom—and break it down into small segments:
   - Walking down the stairs to the room
   - Entering the room
   - Approaching the counter
   - Buying lunch
   - Leaving the counter
   - Looking at the students at the tables
   - Approaching the tables

   Ask the student for help in this breakdown, and ask the student to rank which segment is most anxiety-arousing and which is least. Give rankings to all the other segments as well.

4. Ask the student to relax by systematically relaxing the muscles as taught before. Once the student is breathing deeply and looks relaxed, ask the student to view the memory that is ranked at 0 on the personal anxiety scale. This should be easy to do and cause little anxiety. Ask the student to raise a finger when the image is clear. Then ask the student what ranking he or she would give this image. It should be given a low ranking.

MUSCLE RELAXATION PROGRAM

Ask the student to sit in a very comfortable chair or even to lie on the floor. Ask the student to close his or her eyes. Inform the student that for the next few minutes you will be giving instructions about tightening and relaxing muscles. Ask the student to follow your directions and state that, at the end of the session, the student will feel very relaxed.

Phase One

Start with the legs, and with the left one first. Then repeat the instructions for the right leg. Ask the student to stretch his or her leg out as far as possible. Ask to have the student feel the tension in the muscles, particularly in the thighs and in the foot muscles. Now ask the student to pull the leg back and feel the muscles relax. Ask the student to concentrate on how relaxed this leg feels. Repeat this exercise one more time for the left leg. Now complete the entire exercise for the right leg. Each time, emphasize that the legs are feeling relaxed, very relaxed.

Phase Two

Relax the buttocks. Ask the student to wiggle his or her buttocks in the chair so that there is no tension. Concentrate on reminding the student how relaxed the legs and buttocks are.

Phase Three

Relax the arms. Like the leg exercises, ask the student to alternate by stretching and relaxing each arm muscle. Focus on reminding the student how relaxed the muscles are.

Phase Four

Relax the stomach and chest areas. Ask the student to take a few deep breaths and hold the air. Each time, ask the student to exhale slowly through the nose. As this is done, focus on reminding the student how relaxed his or her whole body is becoming.

Phase Five

Relax the head and neck muscles. Ask the student to twist the neck gently to relieve any tension. Ask the student to twist the nose and raise the eyebrows and to feel the tension in his or her forehead. Repeat these exercises a few times.

Now remind the student how relaxed he or she is feeling, and how heavy his or her arms and legs are. Ask the student to concentrate a few minutes on how relaxed he or she is and, when ready, to open his or her eyes.

Figure 1–9

5. Having tested the technique, the next step is to move to the ranking system the student constructed for his or her specific fear. Ask the student to close his or her eyes and once again relax. Allow about 30 seconds for relaxation to set in. Begin with the lowest ranking of the segments. Ask the student to view the image. Once again, ask for the finger signal. Wait a few seconds, and then ask the student to rank the fear of this image on the 0 to 100 personal anxiety scale. Let us say that Joe ranks as 20 the image of walking into the cafeteria.

    Now repeat this step, using the same image as before. Remember to ask the student to relax and to raise his or her finger when the image is present. Again, ask the student to rank the image on the 0 to 100 scale. This time the image should have a lower rank. Continue with this step until the image receives a 5 or less ranking in anxiety by the student. Usually, three or four repetitions are needed to eliminate the image's anxiety.

6. At the next meeting, usually the next day, the teacher should implement Step 5 with the next segment of the fear image. Continue to ask for a ranking of anxiety for each segment until a level of 5 or less is obtained.

    Gradually, you will eliminate all high-level rankings of anxiety on all the segments, even for the one that caused the highest.

    In our case with Joe, he eventually reached his highest anxiety-level segment—approaching the lunch tables with a tray full of lunch—and reduced the imagery anxiety level to 5.

7. Once you have reached the last segment, inform the student it is now time to test the success of the fear reduction by actually going through that anxiety-arousing behavior. Remind the student of his or her success at reducing the level of fear, and remind him or her to relax before starting out.

Variation of This Procedure

Rather than using internal imagery to help a student reduce a fear-arousing experience, use the procedure described above but have the student actually carry out fear reduction in a real situation.

HOW TO USE OTHER STUDENTS TO HELP IMPROVE A STUDENT'S BEHAVIOR

Are there times when no matter what you do, how long you try, or how hard you work, nothing positive happens to improve a student's behavior? You may even wonder if the student needs to be placed in another class before he or she destroys the order and classroom atmosphere you have worked to create. If such is the case, then perhaps it is time you call in the great "equalizer" of classroom management procedures—group pressure.

There are a number of classroom management procedures that employ group pressure to motivate students to conform to the accepted group norm. For most children, what the group thinks, feels and does assumes monumental proportions when he or she is deciding how to act. The key for you is to direct these group norms to support your classroom norms. Once you have crafted this merger, you can apply group pressure to motivate a student to change. It is extremely difficult for a disruptive student to continue his or her behavior when the rest of the class is working in the other direction. If a student does manage to resist this pressure and still continues to disrupt, then you have clear evidence that this student does not belong in your class. A student who is so limited mentally or disturbed emotionally that he or she can deny or resist the group pressure to conform behaviorally will also reject the academic goals of the class.

Below are listed a number of classroom management procedures that employ group pressure strategies. They each can and should be adapted to fit the needs of the student in your particular classroom.

Behavior Teams (BT)

This procedure uses teams of students competing against each other to demonstrate the least number of disruptions. The class is divided into teams in such a manner that the teams are composed of a mix of students. In a class of 12 students, for example, there might be four teams of three students each. Place a seriously disruptive student on a team that contains a student who is strong socially and who is seen as a leader. In this manner, the disruptive student is pitted directly against the influence and power of another student. If you do not have a positive influential leader in your class, then place the most disruptive student on a team that , you feel, will accept him or her as a team member but not as the leader. Never place all of the most disruptive students on the same team. If you do, you will find that they only reinforce each other and may even withdraw from the game.

The object of the behavior teams is to have accumulated the least number of counts of a specific disruptive behavior. The team members encourage, support, and even reprimand a fellow team member to ensure that the team, as a group, receives the least number of counts. A prize is usually given at the end of the week consisting of food, objects suited to the age level of the child, extra school privileges, such as more free time, less homework, or even the right to be first in the lunch line. Teams often assume names, such as the "Challengers," "He-Men," "Boxers," and "The Winners"

From your previous class observations, select *one* disruptive behavior that needs to be managed. Define this behavior in very specific terms so that both you and your students understand what needs to be done. A couple of examples are listed here:

- *Talkouts:* When a student calls out an answer or comment without first raising his or her hand
- *Hitting:* When a student physically touches another with sufficient force to cause hurt
- *Throwing paper:* When a student tosses paper, a book, or a classroom object into the air so that he or she will not be able to catch it.

Before you begin, take a day or two to count the frequency of the specific behavior you have chosen. This simple counting will tell you two things:

1. How prevalent the behavior is in your classroom
2. Whether, after a few days of treatment, the BT's are actually working to reduce the disruption

Introduce the BT concept to your students by using a statement, such as the one described below:

"Today, boys and girls, we will be playing a special game. The game will be going on all day long. You will be placed on a team. Yes, a team, with other students. Once this is done, I will ask each team to try to be the winner—the best. I will be counting how often each of your team members gets out of his or her seat (or whatever the particular target behavior may be). The team with the lowest number at the end of the day (class period, fifteen minutes, or whatever) will be officially declared the winner of this BT game. This team will get the prize."

You will find that students on a particular team exert enormous pressure on each other to produce the least number of occurrences of the specific behavior. Group pressure and the attainment of a reward are powerful dynamics influencing a student's behavior.

The prize can be a simple material good, such as a food item or pencil for younger children and free time or a magazine for older children. Social rewards may also be appropriate. A large banner in the classroom declaring the winners or a formal ceremony of hand-clapping and certificates may be appropriate.

You may also want to use BT to reinforce good or positive behavior as well. For example, you could select on-task behavior, hands-up behavior, and coming-prepared behavior as specific behavior you would like to increase among students.

After a few days of the BT game you should assess your progress. compare team counts to the behavior counts you had established prior to the game. You should have been able to reduce the number of disruptions. You should compare team progress as well. Every team should have a chance to win. If the winning is favoring only a few teams, then reorganize your teams. Eventually, all teams should be reorganized to avoid cliques from becoming established.

In summary, this procedure works for both younger and older students. You may need to change the orientation to meet your class needs, but you will find this procedure does produce positive results rather quickly.

The Lottery

Lotteries are very popular today. Even the youngest child understands how they work. A lottery can also be used as an efficient, effective method to reduce disruptive behavior. In this system, students earn tickets, actual lottery tickets, for demonstrating positive behavior. At the end of a certain period, day, week, or month, the teacher picks a winning ticket. The obvious advantage to a student is to gain as many lottery tickets as possible to increase his or her chance of winning. The advantage to a lottery system is that it reduces the number of rewards a teacher needs to purchase, it is time-efficient for a teacher, and it rewards students intermittently, thus increasing anticipation.

To introduce this procedure, say something like this to the students.

"Today the lottery is in effect. The grand drawing will be on Friday, and the winner will receive a lunch at Burger King (or some other reward). How do you win? It is easy. First, you need a ticket with your name on it. This ticket will be placed in the drum along with all the tickets other students may have. The one chosen wins. How do you get a ticket? I give out the tickets. I only give tickets out to students who bring in their homework (or whatever behavior you choose). You can receive as many tickets as possible. The more days you bring in homework, the more tickets and, therefore, the better chance you have of winning. The lottery starts now. Any questions?"

You will need to define specifically what it is the students need to do to receive a lottery ticket. As with previous procedures, you need to define what it is that you mean. In our example, you would need to define "homework."

This lottery system can be used on a wide variety of behaviors. Some of the research has shown positive student behavior in areas of class attendance, in-seat behavior, swearing, coming prepared, talking without permission, and hand-raising. For whatever behavior you are attempting to change, it is a good idea to first count the frequency with which it occurs before you attempt the lottery. The baseline, as in the BT procedure, provides you with a reference point of see if the lottery does indeed reduce a disruptive behavior or increase a positive behavior.

If you find no change or little change in behavior after a week, then you need to look at one or both of these factors. First, ask yourself if the students understand what they need to do. Is the behavior specific and to the point? Next, ask yourself if the reward is attractive enough and if it is given soon enough to be motivating. Sometimes, you will need to conduct the lottery every day or every few days so that the students are motivated sufficiently to be rewarded.

Dot-to-Dot

This procedure can be used with younger and older children alike. First, you need to find someone handy on your staff who can draw. If no such person exists, then you could use trace paper to complete the project. You need to compose a picture, individualized for each class, fashioned out of a dot matrix. To complete the picture, the class needs to draw a line from dot to dot. The picture can be an easy one for younger children (10 dots) and much more difficult for older children (100 dots). There is no set criteria. Place a much larger dot for every three dots for younger children and for every 15 dots for older children. This larger dot is the reward dot. You may need to adjust the frequency of these larger dots to make them easy to attain. The picture needs to be attractive enough to interest a child to complete. Cartoon characters, heroic and doll-like figures, cars, food and clothes can be attractive items.

Like the other two procedures in this section, you need to define for the students a particular behavior you want to decrease or increase. Take, for example, completing one's workbook pages. You need to tell the students that, for every assignment completed in the workbook, you will allow those students finished to draw a line between two dots. There may be five students who finish the first time. These five can draw a line. When the large dot is reached, everyone receives a reward in the class. The reward can be material or social.

The key to this procedure is that the students are motivated to complete the picture and to receive the reward. The greater the number of students completing the assignment, the faster the class reaches its goal. No one is penalized for not receiving the reward. However, other students in the class will put pressure on a student to conform to the task, because, first, they want to get to the big dots quickly and, second, they have a sense of fair play. If a student in the class is not helping, then that student should not receive the reward. It is very difficult for a single student from a class to resist this subtle and, often, not so subtle pressure.

Public Goal Setting

There is a procedure that can dramatically decrease negative behavior and increase positive behavior without the use of rewards. Sounds too good to be true? There are advantages at times to display and to make public a student's performance if you seek quick behavior change without the involvement of rewards. While the three procedures discussed earlier also employ public goal setting, this procedure does not hide the fact that group pressure is being employed to change behavior. While it can be embarrassing to some students, it can also be very rewarding to others.

To implement this procedure, you first need to meet with every child in your class individually. Discuss with him or her what behavior you would like changed and why. Be specific and honest here . For example,

> "Stanley, you need to remain in your seat longer during workbook assignments. By that I mean you need to remain seated at your desk. You got out of your desk ten times in the half hour we had workbook time yesterday. While I know you think all these out-of-seat behaviors were for a good reason, they are annoying me. I want you to change. Can we reduce this out-of-seat behavior somewhat?"

Here Stanley is given the opportunity to get his own goals. The teacher is not asking him to give up completely the out-of-seat behavior, because that probably would be an impossibility. Rather, the teacher is asking him to change. The process here should allow Stanley to reduce his out-of-seat behavior. Stanley may choose five out-of-seat behaviors for the next workbook assignment period. The teacher needs to judge whether the student's choice is a sufficient change to reduce the problem and whether the change will be challenging enough to the student.

Once the teacher has developed specific goals for every student in the class, the time has come to post behavior performance charts. These are charts that each student will use to record publicly his or her behavior. Figure 1-10 is an example of Stanley's chart.

You can see that over the period of the past three days, Stanley has managed to reduce his out-of-seat behavior. To complete his chart, the teacher records the number of times Stanley was out of his seat during the workbook period. At the end of the period, Stanley is told his number and asked to put his mark on the chart representing his progress or lack of progress. Other students during the day are requested to fill in their charts also. At the end of the day, the teacher could ask students in the class who made progress and who did not.

As you can see, this form of charting is very public. The fact that others are watching, comparing, is a powerful motivation to change.

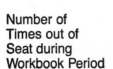

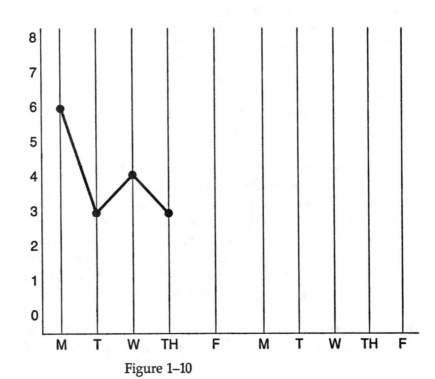

Figure 1–10

HOW TO CONTROL THE BEHAVIOR
OF AN ANGRY, DISRUPTIVE
STUDENT

As you read this section, you will be able to identify and understand the behavior of many angry children you have known. You will be able to use this understanding of these children to help you deal in the future with any other angry children you have yet to encounter. I strongly suggest that you take time to read and reread this section. Understand it thoroughly. When you need to utilize its contents at some future date you will need to recall it quickly and efficiently. One thing angry, disruptive children do not allow you is time to cope with them. So be prepared, and spend extra time reading this section.

Let's begin by talking about our terms, "control," "angry," and "aggressive." What do we mean by these? Control has two different strategies attached to it. The first is simple recognition or awareness of anger, and the second is management to change the direction of anger. Each of these two strategies will be explained as they relate to dealing with an angry student.

First, let's begin with a word about anger and aggression. Anger and aggression are different emotions. Anger is a temporary state, usually associated with being frustrated or hurt. Aggression is anger turned into rage with an intent to hurt a person or to destroy school property. Dealing with either of these emotional states is not easy. With regard to anger, our culture does not train us to recognize our own feelings of anger, how to accept them, and how to deal with them. Therefore, we often have great difficulty recognizing, accepting, and dealing with feelings of anger in others. In fact, people who are angry near us can often trigger our own anger. Many times, you can actually hear this happen. When a student starts shouting at a teacher, the teacher will gradually increase the intensity in his or her own voice to the point where there is a corresponding anger. (Aggression is not discussed here but is dealt with in the next strategy described in this chapter.)

There are two characteristics of anger that need to be defined before recognition and management strategies are discussed.

- *Form:* The form of anger can either be inactive or passive form. The active form usually is manifested by being loud, sarcastic, abusive, and blaming. The passive form is characterized by hesitancy, questioning, lowered voice, and acceptance of fault for the problem.
- *Direction:* The direction of a student's anger can be either toward you or away from you. It is usually much easier to deal with a student who is angry at someone else than it is dealing with a student directing his or her anger at you.

Combining these two aspects of anger, form and direction, it is possible to classify most student anger into one of four states. These are listed here with examples:

1. *Active anger directed at you—*

> HELEN: You are the most boring teacher I have had. I hate you. I am going to get you someday.

2. *Active anger directed at another—*

> TERRY: The principal needs to be taken care of. The idiot took my radio.

3. *Passive anger directed at you—*

> HELEN: How come you always pick on me? Do you hate me?

4. *Passive anger directed at another—*

> TERRY: I probably will get suspended by the principal for bringing in my radio box. I'm not going to talk to him.

In order of difficulty, we have the most difficulty dealing with Example 1, active anger directed at us, and the least difficulty dealing with Example 4, passive anger directed at another. If you look back at how students demonstrated their anger, you could probably classify each of these occasions under one of the four types described here. Further, you might take a few minutes and look over your present class of students, and decide which state of anger each student displays most often. Form 1-6 will help you in this process.

A discussion follows of the strategies you will need to adopt in order to control these four anger states. The first is the recognition and awareness stage; the second is the management stage.

Recognition Stage Strategies

Many students become angry, and they do not know it. They just act in a hostile manner without awareness of the feelings behind these acts. You cannot help a student control his or her anger if the student is unaware of the anger. To help a student become aware, you need to reflect the displayed anger back to the student. You do this verbally. For example, this active anger statement directed at you could be handled this way:

> LYNN: I am tired of you and your nice talk.
> TEACHER: You are angry at me.
> [Here the teacher reflects the anger back to Lynn and tells her she is angry.]

ANGER CLASSIFICATION CHART

State   *Student(s)*   *Incident*

1. Active anger directed at you:

   _____

   _____

   _____

   _____

2. Active anger directed at another:

   _____

   _____

   _____

3. Passive anger directed at you:

   _____

   _____

   _____

   _____

4. Passive anger directed at another:

   _____

   _____

   _____

   _____

Form 1-6

LYNN: You're damn right I am.
[Lynn confirms this anger.]

In the case of a passive anger statement directed at you, you might say:

TOMMY: I do not want to talk about it.
TEACHER: You are angry with me, and you don't want to talk to me.
[Reflected feelings.]
TOMMY: Yeah.
TEACHER: What is it about me that causes you so much anger?
[Here the teacher is inviting Tommy to talk about his anger. The message given is that anger is okay to express.]

A second recognition strategy is to inform or educate students themselves about the four different anger states. Ask the students to give examples of each state from their own lives or from events that happened in the class or in the school. Students can even role-play examples of each state. If you are really brave, ask them to give examples of when you were exhibiting anger of the various states. The goal here is to make students aware of anger and how it manifests itself. Later, when a student displays anger, you can refer back to the information you have provided to help with rapid access to the recognition stage.

One difficulty many teachers have with the recognition stage is that they themselves have great difficulty dealing with anger from another. Therefore, it is very difficult to recognize this anger when it is demonstrated. As a result, teachers make mistakes in the recognition stage and label anger as something else, or they even deny its existence altogether. We all display examples, such as those listed below, from time to time. Being aware of our errors will perhaps help us not to repeat them so frequently:

- *Probing:* Here a teacher tries to find out the reasons the student is angry even before anger is recognized as existing. Often, the teacher guesses. For example, "You are upset because of the grade I gave you."

- *Denying:* Here the teacher tells the student he or she is not angry. "You are not angry," or, "You should not be upset."

- *Inserting:* Here the teacher inserts other feelings rather than allowing anger to exist. This especially happens with passive forms of anger when the hostility is not so readily detected. "You seem confused here," or, "You seem hurt" are typical responses rather than the proper, "You are angry here."

- *Blaming:* Here the teacher tells the student he or she is wrong to be angry at the teacher. The anger is passed off onto someone else. For example, "You should not be angry at me. The rules are the rules. I did not write them."

Management Stage Strategies

The purpose of these strategies is to help the students develop their own control methods to deal with anger. Having first helped the student recognize and be aware of his or her anger, you now are ready to go the next step to help the student use this anger in a positive way.

View the student's anger in neutral terms if you can. While the anger may seem antagonistic, bitter, hostile, assaultive, and hurting to you, it also can have qualities of tension reduction, problem resolution, value clarification, goal and role clarification, and even classroom stabilization. You can use a student's anger to move ahead with the student in the social, emotional, and academic tasks ahead.

ACTIVE ANGER.   Teach the student to formalize his or her anger in a verbal statement, take ownership of the anger, and state why he or she is angry and what needs to be done. Here is such an example:

Billy is mad at Mary because she threw his spelling workbook on the floor.

> BILLY: Mary, I am mad   (Ownership statement)
> at you because you   (Why-he-is-angry statement)
> threw my book down,   (Why... statement)
> and I want you   (What-needs-to-be-done statement)
> to say you are sorry.

Here, Billy is being very clear about his anger. He has stated it, admits it openly, and demands action. There is no aggressiveness in this statement, just assertiveness. This formula is easily taught to students of all ages. Here are other examples

Anne is upset, because Marylou told David that Anne likes him.

> ANNE: I am mad because you told. Say you are sorry.

James is mad at Pat because she called him an idiot.

> JAMES: I am very mad because you called me names. Tell me you won't do it again.

Sue is angry at her teacher.

> SUE: You annoy me. I want you to lay off for awhile.

PASSIVE ANGER.   For a student expressing many passive statements, you may need to follow the steps outlined in Figure 1-11. In general, passive angry students do not verbalize their feelings much, so there is a need in management to draw these feelings out slowly, moving from the nonverbal to the verbal.

STEPS FOR GETTING A STUDENT TO VERBALIZE ANGER

Step 1:
Attend and Define Role

Ask the student to talk to you for a few minutes each day about his or her behavior. Make sure this is a private talk. The student may not maintain eye contact with you during this time. He or she may attend to things in your classroom or office more than to you. This could be a test for the teacher. The student may get involved playing with or using some object or toy in the room rather than talk to you. He or she may even steal things while you are not looking. The student expects you to reject him or her. The best strategy is to set limits for the student. Tell him or her what is acceptable and what behavior is not. Also, inform the student what you are trying to do. For example, "Tom, I am trying to help you here. I realize you are angry. I would like to talk to you about this. Perhaps we can work something out."

Step 2:
Talk about What He or She Explores

Nonverbal students like to talk best when they are occupied. Once a student attends to an object, start talking about it. You might comment on a pencil a student picks up by saying, "What do you think of that pencil?" Younger children like puzzles and toys. Older children like checkers, chess, photo albums, and magazines about their age-related interests. Whatever it is, talk with the student about the object.

Step 3:
Talk about the Student

The more the student talks, the more you should reflect back to what the student reveals about him- or herself. This may take time, but as the student begins to trust you, he or she will allow you to make personal comments, such as, "You know, Jim, every time you throw those books back into your desk, I wonder just what it is you are angry about."

Figure 1–11

Step 4:
The Nonverbal Is Replaced

At this point, the student trusts the teacher enough to talk about personal feelings. The student does not need to engage in play or games to deal with his or her feelings. The recognition of feelings, especially that of anger, is easier now and can be verbalized. The time you have set aside for talking should at this step be spent talking about the student's anger and how he or she can best handle it.

Figure 1-11 (continued)

SHARED ACTIVE ANGER.   For two students who are actively angry at each other, you may need to manage their attempt to work out the problem by defining a few rules. Here the anger is recognized but needs direction to be resolved. The following are a few rules to offer:

1. One person talks at a time
2. No physical contact
3. No talking about the past, other than the incident in question
4. No attacking personalities
5. No mind-reading by trying to guess what the other is thinking
6. Deal only with what happened.
7. Leave others out of it
8. No silent treatment, such as refusing to respond to each other
9. Do not presume you know everything that happened

The next step is to have the students frame statements in the form of the first management strategy described. Remind them that nobody leaves your office or classroom until a resolution is reached that is mutually acceptable.

ACTIVE-PASSIVE ANGER.   This is a group technique that allows students to express their anger in a nonverbal mode. Make three small flags that can be mounted at the front of the classroom. One flag of green cloth will represent "no anger"; a flag of yellow cloth will represent the "potential for anger"; and the flag of red cloth will represent "active anger." Inform the students that, at any time during the day, they may go to the flag position and change the green to another color flag when they feel angry. Once they change flags, everyone in the room will be aware of their anger state. Students have the right to discuss or not discuss why they are feeling this way. In either case, the anger is expressed. A student may change the yellow or red flag back to green when he or she feels the anger is calming down. If a yellow or red flag is left displayed at the end of the day, you might want to begin the next day by asking the student if he or she would like to change the flag.

HOW TO AVOID BEING HIT BY AN ASSAULTIVE STUDENT

As you may have already experienced, violence against teachers and students in schools is not a rare occurrence. There is the potential in every school for a student to lose control and become assaultive. When this does occur, there usually is an ugly scene with one or more individuals being hurt. While this book teaches discipline and classroom management strategies to prevent disruptions and destructiveness from destroying the academic climate of your classroom, there are times when all that you do fails. The anger in a student reaches the threshold of control and explodes in an assualtive act.

The strategy discussed here will not teach you how to stop a student from being assaultive. It will, however, teach you some procedures to follow when you are in the proximity of assault behavior or when you are the object of an assaultive act. It is hoped that, if nothing else, you avoid becoming a victim.

The first step, if you have not done so already, is to read the strategy discussed in an earlier section entitled, "How to Control the Behavior of an Angry, Disruptive Student." This strategy will give you some steps to follow first when dealing with student anger. If you follow these steps, you may prevent the angry student from becoming the assaultive student.

Below is a description of an assaultive act upon a teacher. An analysis of this actual event will provide you some guidelines to follow during an assault.

Eric came into the classroom at 8:03 a.m. as soon as the opening bell rang. He threw open the door, yelled a profanity, and threw his scarf on his desk. Other students came in behind Eric with their usual early morning excitement. The teacher decided to confront Eric immediately. He went up to Eric and asked him to step out into the hall. Eric said no. The teacher again demanded that Eric return to the hall. The other students in the class became interested in the verbal confrontation. The teacher held Eric by the arm and said, "Let's go into the hall." Eric threw his book bag at the blackboard, swore again, and ran out of the room. Again, the teacher decided to continue to confront Eric, went out into the hall, and walked after Eric. Eric ran down the hall to the gym. Other students were in the hall at this time and decided to follow what they saw as "serious action." The teacher found Eric waiting outside the gym. The teacher asked Eric why he swore. Eric said nothing. The teacher again asked Eric why he swore and why he ran down the hall. Eric said he had to get his rings from the locker in the locker room. The teacher demanded that Eric go to the main office. Eric said he had to get into the locker room. The teacher demanded that Eric go to the principal's office. Eric slapped the teacher. At this time, another student jumped at Eric and pulled him down the hall away from the teacher. The teacher turned to the crowd of 70 or so students and asked them to return to class. The student who had intervened with Eric said she would take Eric to the principal's office. The teacher thanked the student and returned to class. The final episode of this story was played out at a superintendent's hearing, at which Eric was suspended from school. The Committee on the Handicapped met and, after a review of the records, transferred Eric to a more restrictive environment.

Scenes like the one just described are ugly indeed. Neither the teacher nor the student understood how the events reached such intensity. Neither wanted it to happen. Neither won. It is possible, however, to look at this scene with a critical eye to determine what went wrong. We will break the scene into six critical acts:

- *Act I: Student Disruption.* Eric demonstrated disruptive behavior by coming into the classroom swearing and yelling.

- *Act II: Teacher Reaction.* The teacher decided to confront this disruption. He issued a verbal command. He asked Eric to step out into the hall.

- *Act III: Student Disruption Continues or Escalates.* Eric chose to ignore the command and escalates the disruption by throwing the bag. Here should have been "warning" lights flashing for the teacher to read. Clearly, this was an ordinary disruptive act escalating, not terminating. There was obviously something fueling Eric's disruptive act. There was something or somebody bothering him.

- *Act IV: Teacher Reacts to the Behavior, Not the Emotion.* The teacher misread the warning lights and viewed the escalation as a challenge to his authority. His behavior started to pace or assume qualities of the student's behavior. The vocal tone became more intense and louder. The nonverbal behavior matched—face-to-face encounters, fists clenched, lips tightly drawn, arms tight, legs separated and anchored. There usually is an ultimatum delivered in Act IV; the teacher demands that the student do something. In our scene, the teacher grabbed Eric, thereby escalating a deteriorating situation even more. When Eric left the room, the teacher responded by going after him.

- *Act V: Panic Sets In.* At this point, both the student and the teacher refused to back down. The ego or pride of each participant becomes fused with the behavior. Neither knows how to get out of a situation that has gotten out of control. One or both may be conscious of this panic, but the speed of events usually eliminates the time to think it through. Silence during Act V is not used nor read as de-escalation. Rather, silence becomes time for the teacher to make quantum leaps. In our case, the time it took for Eric and the teacher to run through the hall and the consequent silence added significantly to the tension. Neither Eric nor the teacher were backing down now.

- *Act VI: Explosion.* This is the final act in a tragic series of events. At this point, the tension is so intense that neither the student nor the teacher can handle it. The result is a release in an explosive act. Usually, the behavior is one of fight or flight by either the teacher or the student. If fight behavior is manifest, the teacher or the student will assault the other. If flight behavior is engaged, either the teacher or the student will flee from the scene. In our scene, Eric decided to fight. He struck the teacher. This explosion released his tension. Fortunately, a student intervened and prevented a potential major brawl. The teacher quickly regained composure and took charge of the situation in order to defuse it. Note that the explosion can also be in the form of shouting and swearing; especially with younger children, the teacher can "chew" the student out by assaulting him or her verbally.

There were other aspects in our example that need to be addressed. First, there was the problem of peer pressure. While this dynamic does not exist in every assaultive act, when it does, it can be like gasoline on a flame. Was Eric playing to the other students? Were some of them encouraging him on? How could the teacher have backed down without losing face? Second, there was the issue of Eric's preoccupation to get into the locker room to retrieve his rings. Was he angry that he lost them, could not get at them, and was prevented from getting to them? The rings were certainly part of the morning pressures. Third, when Eric left the room was he avoiding (fleeing) a potential assaultive act? Could it have ended there? While we do not know answers to these questions, we do know there was more involved in this assault than a student hitting a teacher.

How could this teacher avoid being hit? Here are some suggestions the teacher could have implemented to decrease the tension, avoid the assault, and deal with the child's anger:

- When the scene reached Act III, the teacher should have realized the warning signals. The student was escalating the disruption, not calming down.

- At Act IV, the teacher should have reacted to the emotion, the anger, that Eric was displaying, not the behavior. For example, the teacher could have said, "Gee, Eric, you are very angry this morning. Do you want to talk about it?"

- Ask the student to leave the scene. This would have bought Eric time to calm down without the teacher being present. In this case, Eric could have been sent to a time-out room or to the principal's office.

- Ask another student to help you by taking Eric to the office, by talking to Eric in the hall, or by telling you what was bothering Eric.

- If the situation still reached act V, where panic was present, the teacher should have walked away. As long as Eric was not threatening another student, himself, or attempting to destroy school property, the teacher could have left the scene. He then could have gone to get a principal or a fellow teacher to help Eric de-escalate. School disciplinary action could still be imposed on Eric by the administration. It is better here to lose the battle and to win the war.

In summary, let it be said that in most cases there are very predictable stages to an escalating assaultive situation. If a teacher is aware of these various stages, he or she can have some control on the escalation process. If nothing else, they should serve as warning lights that something serious is wrong. A few suggestions are made here to help a teacher cope with the escalating steps. While we can all learn using hindsight from such a situation, there is also the realization we can learn to prevent its repetition.

It is not the scope of this book to teach teachers how to handle or intervene with physically assaultive students. The skills necessary to deal with an actual physical assault need to be learned by actual demonstration. Figure 1-12 gives descriptions of two consulting groups that provide this intensive training.

TRAINING PROGRAMS IN PHYSICAL RESTRAINT AND PROTECTION FROM ASSAULTIVE STUDENTS

Non-Abusive Physical and Psychological Intervention (NAPPI)

> 250 Minot Avenue
> P.O. Box 473
> Auburn, Maine 04210
> (207) 782-0074
> (800) 343-1394, extension 13

NAPPI training is designed for school personnel working with emotionally disturbed, learning disabled, or multiple handicapped students with problems of impulsiveness, assaultiveness, or aggressive behavior. NAPPI methods help students regain self-control while avoiding injury and abuse to self and others. The training enables staff control without loss of therapeutic impact or violation of the relationship. The training focuses on assessment, prevention, and intervention techniques, as well as the therapeutic use of physical restraint devices. NAPPI methods are used extensively in this country and Canada and are easily learnable by a wide range of staff. Specially trained children (SMART Kids) as trainers may be used to help the staff learn about the special problems involved.

> National Crisis Prevention Institute (CPI)
> 4011 W. Capitol Drive
> Milwaukee, Wisconsin 53216
> (800) 558-8976

CPI has been providing individuals and institutions with the practical "how-to" techniques and skills to handle effectively the most demanding behavior crises. The resulting improvement in confidence and morale of providers means better care for the disruptive individual. Participants will learn among other things to identify the potential for violent or disruptive behavior, reduce tensions, prevent violent episodes, intervene safely in violent situations, and maintain effective staff operation during a crisis.

Figure 1–12

CHAPTER 1 REFERENCES

Curwin, Richard L., and Allen N. Mendler. *The Discipline Book: A Complete Guide to School and Classroom Management.* Reston, VA: Reston Publishing, 1980.

Grossnickle, Donald R., and Frank P. Saks. *Promoting Effective Discipline in School and Classrooms; A Practitioner's Perspective.* Reston, VA: National Association of Secondary School Principals, 1985.

Harris, Karen R. "Definitional, Parametric, and Procedural Considerations in Timeout Interventions and Research." *Exceptional Children, 51,* 4, 279-288, 1985.

Howard, Eugene R. *School Discipline Desk Book.* West Nyack, NY: Parker Publishing, 1978.

Kelly, Marylou, and Trevor F. Stokes. "Contingency Contracting with Disadvantaged Youths: Improving Classroom Performance." *Journal of Applied Behavior Analysis, 15,* 447-454, 1982.

Maurer, Richard E. *Elementary Discipline Handbook: Solutions for the K-8 Teacher.* West Nyack, NY: The Center for Applied Research in Education, 1985.

Somers, Joann, Michael Verdi, Philip Bourbeau, and Martin Sheen. "Teaching Job Independence and Flexibility to Mentally Retarded Students Through the Use of Self-Control Package." *Journal of Applied Behavior Analysis, 18,* 81-85, 1985.

Wolpe, Joseph, and Arnold Lazarus. *Behavior Therapy Techniques: A Guide for the Treatment of Neuroses.* New York: Pergamon Press, 1966.

chapter 2

ADVANCED TECHNIQUES FOR CHANGING STUDENT BEHAVIOR

What makes this chapter different from the first chapter is that it asks the teacher to become involved with the thinking process and communication patterns of a student. That is why the strategies of behavior change described in this chapter are referred to as "advanced." Rather than being satisfied with the external evidence of behavior change required in Chapter 1, this chapter offers techniques that require students to change their internal mode of thinking about and solving problems.

Behavior change is more immediate and easier to accomplish using the procedures in Chapter 1. If Chapter 2 procedures are used, the behavior change is apt to be more enduring and of a better quality, even though it takes longer to produce. The strategies in this chapter will appeal to many teachers. The procedures here that force students to engage in a cognitive thinking process to produce behavior change are similar to the procedures a teacher uses to help students produce a change in how they learn academic tasks. A teacher who has studied critical thinking and problem-solving techniques will find this chapter familiar in direction and format. Likewise, a teacher will be able to use the stategies in this chapter regardless of the mental ability of the students. For students possessing very low academic ability, however, a teacher may need to adapt some of these procedures. Regardless, once a teacher has tried the stategies in this chapter, there will be significant change in how students think about problems, how they communicate about them, and most important, in how they behave.

HOW TO TEACH STUDENTS SELF-INSTRUCTION SKILLS TO REDUCE DISRUPTIVE BEHAVIOR

In Chapter 1, a student self-control technique was described that employed the use of behavior modification techniques. There was limited student/teacher dialogue as the emphasis was on student-charting and counting the presence or absence of a particular behavior.

The technique described here is also a student self-control procedure, but it emphasizes the use of verbalization skills over those of charting and counting. Basically, it teaches students to think about what they are doing, to make comments about doing it while they are actually performing a task, and to complete successfully the desired task. Like the procedure described in Chapter One, there are many inherent advantages to teaching students self-control strategies:

- The teacher does not have to monitor the change progress of every student in the room.
- The teacher does not have to reward the student each time the task is completed successfully.
- The student can more easily transfer success in a school setting to one of a nonschool setting by applying self-control procedures.

Teaching Self-Instruction

Self-instruction is a process in which students verbalize directions, either overtly or privately, as they proceed through a task completion exercise. The initial response to a situation is delayed until the student works through a thinking-out-loud strategy. For example, Dorothy always would spit on Armand when he started to tease her about her mother. The teacher response to this altercation was to send the children to a time-out room in the building. After some training, however, the teacher decided to teach Dorothy how to self-control her impulsive need to spit on Armand. To do this, she asked Dorothy to use a self-instruction strategy. After a short period of training, Dorothy was able to cope with Armand's teasing by saying to herself the following:

> "Okay, he did it again. Fine. I can handle this. I will now assert myself and say the following to him: 'You cannot make me upset today. I feel great.' I do not care how he reacts. I can do well, handling him. Good. Even if I miss a word, I can handle him. Fine. Here I go ... [After she makes her short statement to Armand, she thinks—] Great. I did great. Finished. I feel great."

Here the teacher is using a type of change process often referred to as cognitive behavior modification. The process is a combination of using cognitive skills, such as verbal reasoning, and behavior skills, such as symptom relief and specificity, to modify or change unwanted behavior. Training involves a gradual step-by-step learning process.

In training a student to use this procedure, you should follow these initial steps:

1. *Teacher models and talks.* Model for the student how to do the new behavior while, at the same time, self-instruct yourself regarding what to do.

> TEACHER: Now, Dorothy, I am going to role-play a situation I think you could do to handle Armand's teasing remarks. The behavior I am going to show you is called self-instruction. All you have to do is talk to yourself and tell yourself what to do as you actually go about it. Okay?
>
> DOROTHY: Talk to myself? I'm not crazy.
>
> TEACHER: No, you are not crazy. When we practice this, we'll talk out loud, but when you do this in front of Armand, you can talk privately.
>
> DOROTHY: Like to myself?
>
> TEACHER: Exactly. No one will hear. Ready to practice?
>
> DOROTHY: Okay.
>
> TEACHER: The next time Armand teases you, please do the following. Fold your arms in front of you, and repeat this statement, or something like it, to yourself before you say anything to him. "Okay, he did it again. Fine. I can handle this. I will now assert myself and say the following to him: 'You cannot make me upset today. I feel great.' I do not care how he reacts. I can do well, handling him. Good. Even if I miss a word, I can handle him. Fine. Here I go...." Do you understand?
>
> DOROTHY: Yes, I fold my arms like this and say what you said.
>
> TEACHER: Yes, and then say to him out loud, "You cannot make me feel upset today. I feel great." Then say to yourself, "Great. I did great. Finished. I feel great."

2. *Student role-plays, teacher talks.* At this stage of the training, the student rehearses the self-instruction strategy by performing the new behavior, while the teacher instructs the student with the strategy. In our example, Dorothy would practice turning toward Armand, folding her arms, and pausing a few seconds while the teacher said the statement out loud, and then Dorothy would say, "You cannot make me upset today. I feel great."

3. *Student role-plays, student talks out loud.* Here, the student once again rehearses the self-instruction strategy by performing the task.

4. *Student role-plays, student whispers.* For the third time, the student rehearses the new behavior while whispering the statement to him or herself.

5. *Student role-plays, student talks to self.* The student, for the fourth time, rehearses the new behavior while saying the statement to him or herself privately so no one can hear.

Talking to oneself is giving oneself instructions on how to perform the new behavior. Not only does the strategy provide internal guidance but it also tends to occupy the energy and diminish the impulsivity of the student. Students now pause before they act, because they have to self-instruct or "think out loud" to themselves.

Problem-solving skills, such as problem formation, response practice, new behavior, self-reinforcement, and self-evaluation, can be inherently built into this type of strategy. We are teaching students problem-solving skills without having to define the terms for them formally. This learning process is easy. Using our example of Dorothy, these skills will be illustrated:

Skill	*Dorothy*
Problem formation	"Okay, he did it again. Fine. I can handle this."
Response practice	"I will not assert myself."
New behavior	[To Armand] "You cannot make me upset today. I feel great.
Self-reinforcement	"I can do well, handling him. Fine. Here I go. . . . "
Self-evaluation	"Great. I did great. Finished. I feel great."

Other Examples of "Thinking Out Loud"

THE TURTLE TECHNIQUE.   As described by A. Robin, M. Schneider, and M. Dolnick in their article, "The Turtle Technique: An Extended Case Study of Self-Control in the Classroom," (*Psychology in the School*, 13, 1976: 449-453), this technique is excellent for aggressive younger children. You ask them to assume the turtle position when they become upset. They first place their heads on the desk, close their eyes, and then clench their fists. This procedure is welcomed by most students as fun. The real beauty of the procedure is that it provides the student with something to do immediately, delays the aggressive response, and gives the student some time to think of a more constructive response.

Once the student is in the turtle position, have him or her repeat this statement silently:

"Fine. I can handle this. What can I do here which won't get the teacher upset."
or
"Fine. I can handle this. What can I do to make the teacher proud of me instead of losing control of myself."

Once the student has an answer to his or her own self-instruction, he or she can come out of the turtle position.

ACADEMIC SELF-INSTRUCTION.   You can also use this procedure to help students complete difficult academic tasks. For example, a younger child learning how to do the alphabet could be taught to repeat verbal directions to him- or herself while actually drawing the letter. A right-handed child could say:

> "Okay. I can draw a 'd.' First I make a straight line down. Good. Very nice. Now the hard part. I draw a little loop on the side of the line my pencil is not on. Good. If I make a mistake, it is okay. I can redraw it. Good, I did a nice job."

For an older child who needs to write a paragraph on a particular subject, you might consider the following. Ask the student to pause before beginning, and then repeat this form of self-instruction:

> "I can do a paragraph well. What is the problem or topic here? What two things can I say about it? What are some solutions or examples I can write? Take my time."

For problem-solving:

> "I can do a paragraph well. What is the problem here? What two things can I say about it? What are some solutions? Take my time. Now, I will write. Make sure I reread each sentence before turning in the paper. Good."

For a topic explanation:

> "I can do a paragraph well. What is the topic here? What two things can I say about it? What are some examples? Take my time. Now, I will write. Make sure I reread each sentence before turning in the paper. Good."

HOW TO TEACH STUDENTS TO ACT RESPONSIBLY

The purpose of this technique is to teach students a process to enable them to act responsibly. Often, students act appropriately, maturely, their age, or whatever the term for "good" may be, because they have learned to internalize the rules and regulations of the school. How this process takes place is a long complicated one, since early development, community values, and adult-modeling interweave to mold the values and, ultimately, the behavior of a child. However, when there is a flaw in the developmental process, a child needs additional help to learn how to act responsibly.

The purpose of the strategy discussed in this section is to provide a student with a process he or she can use to learn how to act responsibly. At first, the teacher will need to teach the student how to use the process. With younger children, this teaching will need to be reinforced quite frequently. With older children, however, it is possible to teach students the process and then let them use the method on their own to deal with all kinds of problem situations.

The strategy is adapted from William Glasser's *Reality Therapy* (New York: Harper & Row, 1965) and deals primarily with what a student does. While it focuses on behavior, it also deals with the thinking process of the student. The method taught involves asking the student a number of questions. To answer these questions, a student needs to engage his or her cognitive thinking skills. The questions, used in the proper sequence, force the student first to recall, then evaluate, and then analyze his or her behavior. As the student proceeds through this process, the task becomes one of gaining the necessary skill to choose behaviors that are responsible to self and to the community of the class and school.

The Reality Therapy Procedure

There are four questions to ask a student:

1. What are you doing?
2. How is it helping you?
3. Can we make a plan to change?
4. How did it go?

1. WHAT ARE YOU DOING?   This question helps a student recall what happened to bring him or her to a point where a decision has to be made. Very often, this something is a set of behaviors that has resulted in a negative situation. For example, Andy has pulled the chair out from under Mandy. Andy now is in trouble for disrupting the class and for hurting Mandy. The teacher has pulled Andy aside and has asked the question, "What are you doing?"

To answer this question, Andy will need to bring the situation to consciousness. By asking Andy to recall the incident in detail, the teacher will gain a full understanding of what happened. In addition, the student will have the details fresh in his or her mind so the next series of questions can be asked. Here are two examples of how this question can be used.

TEACHER: Andy, what are you doing?
    ANDY: Nothin'. Just having fun.
TEACHER: Tell me what you did?
    ANDY: Well, I just was teasing.

    TEACHER: How did you tease? What happened?
    ANDY: I pulled Mandy's chair out.

The second example follows:

    TEACHER: What are you doing?
    KAY: Homework.
    TEACHER: What kind of homework?
    KAY: You know, that history stuff.
    TEACHER: How much have you done?
    KAY: One question.
    TEACHER: How long have you been at it?
    KAY: Oh, about an hour.
    TEACHER: So you have done one question in an hour.

    2. HOW IS IT HELPING YOU?   This question asks the student to evaluate his or her behavior. Many students do not stop to analyze their behavior to determine whether or not it is appropriate. To answer this question, a student is forced to look at the behavior just recalled with a critical eye. The point is made here that a student be asked to describe how this behavior is helping you, not when it was done. In Andy's case, pulling the chair out gave him immense pleasure at the moment. However, now with the prospect of facing a suspension, a parent conference, or a trip to the principal's office, the behavior is not so helpful. The pleasure is a thing of the past; the conflict is a thing of the moment. If, because of this question, students can see that their previous actions actually hurt them, they will try to avoid these actions in the future. We continue our dialogue with Andy and Kay:

    TEACHER: How did pulling out Mandy's chair help you?
    ANDY: I loved it.
    TEACHER: Yes, but now, how is it helping you?
    ANDY: What do you mean?
    TEACHER: Well, now you have to face me and, maybe, the principal.
            You also have hurt Mandy. How is it helping you?
    ANDY: [He puts his head down and says nothing.]

At this point Andy realizes that what he did has gotten him in some trouble now. He is now focusing on the present, not what he did a few minutes ago.

    TEACHER: How is doing so little homework in so much time helping
            you?
    KAY: Not much?
    TEACHER: What do you mean?
    KAY: I should have done more.
    TEACHER: How would doing more help you?
    KAY: I would not have you bothering me now.

3. CAN WE MAKE A PLAN TO CHANGE?   This question states that change is not only desirable but also necessary. This is not a request but a demand couched in a question. Moreover, at this point in the process, the student, having seen that the behavior is not helping is seeking a way out of the dilemma. To facilitate this change, ask the student for ideas, or ask if there are friends who can offer assistance. In making a plan, force the student to be as specific as possible in the change process. The balance here is to have the student develop as much of the plan as possible. The plan needs to be the student's, not yours. Here are two illustrations of how to use the question.

> TEACHER: Andy, can we make a plan to change?
> ANDY: What should I do?
> TEACHER: What are you going to do to help yourself out of this problem?
> ANDY: I am open to your ideas.
> TEACHER: They need to be yours.
> ANDY: Well...I could not do it again.
> TEACHER: What about Mandy?
> ANDY: Oh, I'll tell her I'm sorry.
> TEACHER: And how will that help you?
> ANDY: It will get you off my back.
> TEACHER: And that is good?
> ANDY: Isn't it?
> TEACHER: How will it help Mandy?
> ANDY: She'll know I mean it, and I won't do it again.
> TEACHER: Can you sum this plan up and tell me when you are going to do it?

The second illustration follows:

> TEACHER: Can we make a plan to change?
> KAY: You want me to work more?
> TEACHER: How will this help you?
> KAY: Well... I won't talk as much and will get more done in school.
> TEACHER: When will we start?
> KAY: Tomorrow.
> TEACHER: How about today?
> KAY: Okay.

4. HOW DID IT GO?   Always follow up a student's plan to change with a question that forces the student to evaluate his or her behavior. At this point, the student will need to determine if, in fact, the plan's objectives were carried out. You should not punish the student for failing. However, do not give up with the need for the student to accept responsibility for his or her plan to change. If a plan fails, recycle Questions 1 through 3 to determine what went wrong. Always ask the

student to recall, evaluate, and choose new patterns of behavior. If a student does complete a plan successfully, offer praise. Below are examples of how to deal with a student who fails to complete a plan and with a student who successfully completes the task.

> TEACHER: How did it go?
> ANDY: I forgot.
> TEACHER: What did you forget?
> ANDY: To... to tell Mandy.
> TEACHER: How did forgetting help you?
> ANDY: Can't I just forget it?
> TEACHER: How is that going to help you?
> ANDY: Come on. I want you to leave me alone on this.
> TEACHER: How will that help?
> ANDY: I'll be left alone.
> TEACHER: Can we make another plan for you to apologize to Mandy?
> ANDY: Okay, okay. I'll do it.
> TEACHER: When?
> ANDY: Now!
> TEACHER: I am waiting.

With Kay, the dialogue continues:

> TEACHER: How did you do?
> KAY: Very well. I did ten questions.
> TEACHER: Excellent, Kay. You are responsible here. You made a plan and decided to go ahead and just do it.

You can see from the series of these four questions that a student is directed through a process of recalling the behavior, analyzing it, evaluating it, making a plan to change it, and evaluating the outcome. Students report that this process makes them feel compelled to search and analyze alternatives to behavior that is not appropriate.

A student, especially an older one, can internalize these four questions and use the process in situations when a teacher is not present to guide him or her. There are a few no-no's to be aware of in using this strategy. If you keep them in mind, you will have a much greater chance of success:

- *Avoid feelings.* While every action has feelings associated with it and one should not repress these feelings when recalling the event, the feelings usually do not assist in helping a student answer these questions. Feelings are subjective. A student cannot be held accountable for feelings. Feelings are neither right nor wrong—they just are. If you become involved with feelings here, you might find yourself at a dead end at Question 2. Here is an illustration.

TEACHER: How did swearing at the principal help you?
RICHARD: It made me feel good.
TEACHER: Yes, how did it help you?
RICHARD: I told you. I feel great. I finally got him.

To get out of this situation, ask the student to refocus on his behavior. You should recognize the feelings but talk about behavior. Continuing our example from above:

TEACHER: How did swearing help you now? [Focus here is on the behavior and the present.]
RICHARD: Now ... well, I am in trouble now.
TEACHER: So, it does not help you now?
RICHARD: Yes, that's right. I am in trouble now.

- *Avoid the question "Why?"* The usual answer to this question is a feeling response; e.g., "I did it because I feel like it." Also, many students do not know why they do things. They are as confused as you are. To please you, they often give you answers even they do not believe are true. Moreover, knowing the reason why a student does something does not mean you will get a student to change behavior. The primary focus should be on the process of recall, analysis, change, and evaluation.
- *Avoid the past and future.* It is hardest to focus on the present. Students more often would like to talk about what happened in the past or what they will do in the future. The present is a confused state where behavior and feelings are wrapped up in a package of doubt and misdirection. However, if change is going to occur, it needs to start now. Often, you need to remind a student of this. For example:

TEACHER: Tell me how it is going to help you now?
    ROSE: I will be famous with my friends [future-oriented].
TEACHER: How about now?
    ROSE: What do you mean? When I did it, I felt just great.
TEACHER: That was then. How is it helping you now?

The following example illustrates how a student can use this strategy to develop responsibility for his or her own behavior. In our example, Joe has had problems understanding the computer course he is taking. He is afraid of asking for help. He is failing and is confused. His resource room teacher has decided to help him.

TEACHER: What is happening in your computer class [Question 1]?

JOE: Nothing.

TEACHER: What about this failure on the report card? What is going on?

JOE: I do not understand. That teacher tells me computers and I are not meant to be. I am afraid of him.

TEACHER: How does failing help you [Question 2]?

JOE: I don't care. Next month I'll never see him again [future-oriented]. Besides, computers are boring [feeling statement].

TEACHER: Yes, I understand they could be boring [feeling recognition], but how is failing helping you now?

JOE: What do you mean?

TEACHER: Well, you have to face me now. That teacher will probably be on your mind for another month. And, finally, you have been receiving an "F" on your report card. [The teacher here is confronting Joe with facts, dealing with the present, and avoiding feelings.]

JOE: What can I do?

TEACHER: Can we make a plan to change [Question 3]?

JOE: Tell me what to do. [Here, Joe wants the teacher to do the work to develop the plan. Except for younger children, it is best to let the student do some of the work here.]

TEACHER: What would you like to happen?

JOE: I want to pass.

TEACHER: What needs to be done to accomplish this?

JOE: I need to understand the work, and that bum needs to get off my back.

TEACHER: What plan can we develop to help you understand the work? [Here, the teacher avoids the remark about what the teacher can do. Neither the student nor this teacher can control the computer teacher's feelings and behavior.]

JOE: I could get help. I could ask questions. I could stay for extra help.

TEACHER: Fine. Which of these do you want to do?

From here on, the student and the teacher develop a specific plan in which Joe can get help in his computer class. While Joe may not score an "A" in this class, he has developed a responsibility for doing better. The teacher kept the questions on track and avoided the no-no's of feelings, the past, the future, and the question, "Why?"

HOW TO IMPROVE STUDENTS' PERSONAL PROBLEM-SOLVING SKILLS

The fact that many or most handicapped students have personal problems is not unexpected. Looking at how many handicapped students attempt to deal with these problems, however, does reveal a deficit in personal problem-solving skills. How can a student help himself or herself when he or she lacks the resources to do so?

You cannot teach a course on personal problem-solving skills to handicapped students with severe personal problems. The course just will not provide information that can be made personal enough to penetrate the gridlock atmosphere in which so many of these problems exist. Perhaps students will view the information you are providing as help, but they will not be able to apply it to the personal issues at hand.

The solution to this dilemma of improving students personal problem-solving skills without directly teaching the process lies in the use of a more subtle unconscious technique. The process involves the use of reading exercises that are followed by a discussion or written exercises about the material read. This procedure has common characteristics associated with that of bibliotherapy. Students read age- and ability-level appropriate material, and they then interact in a dynamic manner either with the characters, the plot, the setting, or the emotions. Usually, a teacher is needed to guide the student through the process. There is sufficient research to suggest that this process may help students in areas of assertiveness, attitude change, behavior change, and self-concept.

The Technique of Bibliotherapy

If you feel that a student's personal problems are of a nature that the student could benefit from reading about others who share similar problems, this technique may be of use. You should have a good, trusting relationship with the student, agree on the presenting problem (e.g., boy/girl relations, death, peer relations, divorce), and have been shown some evidence that the student wants to talk things out. The selection of the appropriate book or story depends on the presenting problem. Some suggestions could be taken from an excellent resource: Jean A. and John T. Pardeck's *Young People with Problems: A Guide to Bibliotherapy* (Westport, Connecticut: Greenwood Press, 1984). It may be possible to integrate the reading selection into the student's curriculum and even allow any writing exercise that develops out of this process to be part of the regular class curriculum. In this manner, the student is not being punished by being given work to solve personal problems.

Stages of Bibliotherapy

There are three stages to this process of change or to the process of personal problem-solving:

STAGE 1: IDENTIFICATION.   Here, the reader actually sees himself or herself in some of the activities of the main charater. This identification is not a full one, because the reader usually pulls only parts of the character's personality, actions, or emotions from the story with which to identify. If students report that, after reading parts of the story, they find themselves daydreaming about their own particular problems, then you can be assured that some identification has taken place.

STAGE 2: VERBALIZATION.   The reader at this stage of the process starts to become involved with the characters in the story. He or she may want to express his or her feelings about one of the characters. By acting out his or her particular feelings about the story's characters, the student releases some of the emotional feelings attached to his or her own problem. The feelings, however, are not just let loose at random but are structured and directed by the teacher around the story being read. The student not only identifies with the story character but now also experiences and acts on the emotional feelings the story has triggered within.

STAGE 3: INTEGRATION.   The final stage of this process is the one in which the student moves beyond the emotional allegiance with the story to a resolution of the problem presented by the story. The student may or may not want ownership of how the story's character solved the problem, but at least during this stage of the process, the student has developed insight into ways problems of this type could be solved. Perhaps the student will be able to integrate resolution actions taken to solve the story problem into actions needed to resolve his or her own personal problems. With the guided assistance of the teacher, this step is possible and the student comes up with solutions of his or her own.

Figure 2-1 illustrates how the three stages of bibliotherapy are applied to a youngster named Timmy. In this example, the entire process took a month and a half. Time is needed to help the student identify the presenting problem, for the teacher to select an appropriate book, for the student to read the story, for discussions to occur at each stage, for extra activities to be completed to help the student work through each stage, and for a final resolution to occur in the student's own head.

This technique is used by many teachers without it having it be formally referred to as process to help students solve personal problems. It very often occurs when students complete language-arts or English assignments. However, what does occur when the teacher is aware of the identification, verbalization, and integration stages is a formal process that is sequenced to produce direct behavior change.

EXAMPLE SHOWING THE STAGES OF BIBLIOTHERAPY

Timmy has a father who is alcoholic and a mother he rarely sees at night because she tends bar at a local tavern. Timmy is in a sixth-grade, self-contained, special-education class. He is classified as emotionally disturbed because he has severe temper tantrums.

Timmy's teacher asked him to read a short story about a boy who has alcoholic parents. In the story, the boy talks about coming home from school to a lonely house. He fixes his own dinner and mostly watches TV. Sometimes, he does homework. He wakes his mother for work at 4:00 p.m. and doesn't see her until the morning when he is on his way to school. The boy avoids his father because he almost always is in a nasty mood. Timmy likes school most of the time but is always late.

Identification. Timmy identified immediately with the character in this story. Not only was the story line similar but also the emotions of loneliness, fear, and confusion were present. The teacher asked Timmy to write a daily schedule for the character in the story and a daily schedule for himself. Once this was done, Timmy and the teacher had a long discussion about how the two schedules were similar.

Verbalization. To help Timmy at this stage of the process, the teacher asked him to write out a short dialogue the character could have with his mother. In the dialogue, Timmy asks the mother to stay at home more, to look over his homework, and to come to back-to-school nights. A number of discussions took place over this dialogue Timmy wrote. In the process, the teacher helped Timmy clarify and work through his own emotions triggered by this story.

Integration. After about a month of writing and discussion, the teacher asked Timmy to write out a list of suggestions he would offer the main character in this story. The suggestions varied, but a few of them were as follows:

- Write your mother a love letter
- Have your aunt come to school with your mother
- Pin your school work up in the kitchen for your mother to notice

Figure 2–1

Figure 2-2 gives a list of classroom activities, which may help the teacher with ideas to use with each of these stages. These activities are grouped according to the particular stage of problem-solving the student is experiencing. It is advised that the teacher adapt these to meet the age and ability level of the student.

HOW TO TEACH STUDENTS WHY THEY DISRUPT AND ACT OUT

There are many teachers who believe that a student cannot change disruptive behavior without first gaining some insight into "why" he or she acts as he or she

CLASSROOM ACTIVITIES FOR EACH STAGE OF PROBLEM SOLVING

Identification Stage
1. Have the student write a week's diary as the main character in the book might have written it.
2. Have the student take a character in the story who is not the most visible and develop more action for him or her.
3. Have the student draw a cartoon-type script of the story's characters acting out an important phase of the story.

Verbalization Stage
1. Select a sequence from the book, and have the student role-play the action.
2. Have the student write a letter to one of the characters in the book expressing his or her personal opinion of what happened.
3. Have the student take a newspaper or magazine and cut out pictures or words describing the different phases or sequences of the story.
4. Have the student use puppets or finger puppets to act out part of the story.

Integration Stage
1. Have the student write on a piece of paper some advice he or she would give to one of the book's characters. Share this advice in a discussion.
2. Have the student list all of the good qualities and all of the weak qualities of one of the story's characters. Once this is done, have the student give the character a personal quality he or she feels would help the character.
3. Have the student change the ending of the story. Have the students involve another character, scene, or twist of events.

Figure 2–2

does. Perhaps, you are one of these teachers. This technique has as its primary goal the instruction of children in the "whys" of behavior. The secondary goal associated with this procedure is to help children use this new insight to change maladaptive behavior.

The first step in using this technique is to understand the belief system that supports it. Many teachers believe that all students seek recognition from their behavior. When students do not achieve, in their judgment, appropriate recognition, they may pursue other goals. This other goal-seeking behavior has serious consequences for a teacher because it surely will be disruptive.

Take for example this student's need to achieve recognition. The response of the teacher is appropriate and fulfills the student's needs.

> JOAN: Mrs. Smith, is my math workbook okay today?
> MRS. SMITH: Nice work, Joan. You have done well in such a short period of time.
> Perhaps, your columns of numbers could be straighter, however.

In the next example, Joan begins to disrupt the lesson, because she feels that she is not getting appropriate recognition. Whether or not she has is a matter of judgment on the student's part.

> JOAN: Mrs. Smith, you really need to look at this work.
> MRS. SMITH: I have, Joan. It is good but needs to be completed.
> JOAN: Well, I am not going to do it. Kerry has not done a thing.
> If she is not doing it then I am not. Make me.

Before we determine why Joan is acting the way she is, let us present the four possible goals she could be pursuing at this moment. We will then analyze Joan in detail and come up with some behavior-change techniques.

Goals

The four goals a disruptive child could be pursuing are listed here. They are adapted from Rudolf Dreikurs' *Psychology in the Classroom*, pp. 27-29, copyright 1957, 1968 by Rudolf Dreikurs; reprinted by permission of Harper & Row Publishers, Inc.

- Getting attention
- Getting power
- Getting revenge
- Displaying inadequacy

These goals are interrelated in that a child may first act out under the faulty logic that disruption will gain recognition and attention. If this behavior fails, then the child may seek to gain power through another type of disruption. If no satisfaction is gained here, the child may move to the next goal of revenge and eventually to a goal of "leave me alone."

Here are some examples of behavior a child could use to pursue each goal.

1. *Getting attention* (being outspoken, loud, noisy):

    - Lining up to get on the bus, Vinny breaks from the line and starts to run down the sidewalk.

- Linda walks into the classroom while others are working quietly and announces, "I am back everyone."

The more students gain attention this way, the more frequently they try it.

2. *Getting power* (being stubborn, deceitful, arguing):

- Chad refuses to give the principal a cassette tape that contains vulgar music. "It is not mine to give up. I won't, I just won't."
- James hides a fellow student's notebook but will not admit it. "I saw it, but I did not take it. Search me. Call my mother."

These students get a teacher into a power struggle. They win whether or not they get what they want.

3. *Getting revenge* (being violent, passive-aggressive, or sullen):

- William turns to the teacher and says, "I hate you. You have caused more harm than good here. I want our other teacher."

These students expect to be hurt. They win if they are disliked.

4. *Displaying inadequacy* (wanting to be left alone, expecting to fail, feeling hopeless):

- Carolyn plays at being stupid. She doesn't complete her work and refuses to bring in homework.
- Jenny is referred to as a "blob" by her teacher, because she does nothing, displays no motivation, and is failing.

Students at this stage have given up and are so accustomed to failure that they do not care to be tested and fail again.

Intervention

There are three questions to ask a child to start the process of change. The answers to these questions will provide you and the student with an insight into why the student acted the way he or she did to disrupt the class.

QUESTION 1:   Do you know why you [describe the disruptive act]?
The answer to this question is usually "no." Most students truly do not know why they disrupt. If an explanation is given, it could be just a rationalization to throw you off. For example, "I did it because Mary hit me."

QUESTION 2:   Would you like to know? I have some ideas. Most students say "yes" to this question. If they say "no" or if they do not care, then you could assume that the child is pursuing Goal #4 of displaying inadequacy. In either case, present the next question. The student will hear you.

QUESTION 3:   Could it be that when you [describe the disruptive act], you wanted special attention? You wanted to be boss and have it your way? You wanted to hurt others? You wanted to be left alone?

Present all four goals here in a nonjudgmental tone. Let the student figure out which goal he or she is pursuing. Some private logic operates in each one of us, and your questions will connect to the student's logic. You should be observant as you name each goal to see if the student shows some kind of recognition. Usually, the facial features of a student will display whether the student has gained insight into his or her behavior goal. The eyes widen, the mouth opens, and the eyebrows rise when the recognition or insight comes.

If after you have asked these three questions, you are still unsure about the student's goal or goals, then ask yourself how *you* feel. Your feelings will often point to what the student is pursuing. For example:

1. If you are distracted by the student's behavior, the student may be seeking attention.
2. If you are feeling hurt by what the student did or said, then the student may be seeking power.
3. If you are angry at the student, he or she is perhaps seeking revenge.
4. If you are feeling frustrated and annoyed about what a student is not doing, maybe the student is displaying inadequacy and wants to be left alone.

Let us return now and analyze why Joan is acting in such a disruptive manner.

JOAN: Well, I am not doing to do it. Kerry has not done a thing. If she is not doing it, then I am not. Make me.

MRS. SMITH: Do you know why, Joan, you said, "Make me"? [Question #1]

JOAN: Nope.

MRS. SMITH: Would you like to know? I have some ideas. [Question #2]

JOAN: Okay.

MRS. SMITH: Could it be, Joan, that when you said, "Make me," you were wanting special attention? [Pause] Or you were wanting to have it your way? [Pause] Or you were wanting to get even with me? [Pause] Or you just want to be left alone? [Question #3]

> JOAN: [Smiling, showing recognition] I guess I wanted to show you I was boss. What's wrong with that? You always boss me.
>
> MRS. SMITH: So your reason for doing so was to have it your own way and to be boss?
>
> JOAN: Yes!

Action Steps

It is assumed that once a student has insight into why he or she does things that the behavior will change. This is not necessarily as simple as it may seem. One thing that will surely happen, however, is that you will start talking with the student about why this need is so great. The student will receive attention and recognition—a goal originally behind this whole behavior problem.

Listed below are some tips you could use to change behavior once you and the student have identified the goal being sought.

ATTENTION.   Ignore the disruption until the act is over. Provide extra attention and encouragement during nondisruptive moments. Make comments, such as "Gee, Joan, you are a model student now. I just love your working so well. I sure hope you do not go off on one of your attention-seeking tantrums. I will have to ignore you then."

POWER.   Inform the student that he or she is seeking power. Admit the student has power. Comments: "I really cannot make you do the work, Joan. It is up to you to decide or not. Perhaps, you could help me get out of this power struggle with you. Let's agree on something here."

REVENGE.   Apply the logical or natural consequences of the action. Inform the student of what will happen. Inform the student or describe why you like the student. Comments: "Please, Ted, let's be sensible. If you continue to curse at me, I will have to suspend you. Do you really want to go the next step in this confrontation? Do you know what it is? What could I do different to get you to like me?"

INADEQUACY.   Encouragement is the key here. Find small tasks a student could do well, and let him or her attempt them. Go out of your way to say "hello" or "nice going." Ask for the student's input during a class discussion.

HOW TO TEACH STUDENTS NEW WAYS TO INTERPRET EXPERIENCES

Students, like most of us, usually respond to an experience or an event with a behavior that they feel is an appropriate response to the particular circumstances of the event. This is true even when the behavior is disruptive. Wouldn't it be great if we could change perceptions? Perhaps then we would have the students demonstrate behaviors other than disruptive ones. As an example:

Marylou took Anne's lunch from the table and hid it under a coat. When Anne came looking for her lunch, she became upset and started to thrash books, coats, and chairs about looking for it. In the process, she spilled her food on the floor. Marylou just laughed and thought the whole matter was hilarious. Anne, however, became more anry and called Marylou an obscene name. Marylou responded by slapping Anne. Soon, a fist fight erupted in the cafeteria between the girls.

Looking at the two girls' responses to the escalating tension, it may be hard to figure out why they took the whole matter so seriously and why it had to come down to a fight. To be sure, in each of these girl's eyes, the behavior they chose to respond to seemed to be appropriate, if not justified, because of the action of the other. Anne may have viewed the situation as one of losing face in front of her friends. To be tricked by Marylou's prank was embarrassing to her. For Marylou, the view of the situation was one of comic relief. The more Anne became upset, the more humorous the situation became to Marylou. Anne's use of an obscene name, however, changed the comic to the hurt, and Marylou may have viewed the hurt as too much to handle. She felt she had to hurt Anne to keep the leadership of the event, so she escalated the verbal hurt to one of physical hurt.

If we want to generalize, most disruptive acts seen in their context, can be considered an appropriate reponse. This is a powerful statement. It bears repeating. Most disruptive acts, seen in their context, can be an appropriate response.

The key condition, as stated, is the context of the situation. It is not necessarily the right perception or the only perception, but in the student's eyes it is the only one. Anne saw herself as being embarrassed by the prank; that was her only view of the event. The disruptive behavior she chose to deal with the event was appropriate. So, in Anne's view, calling Marylou an obscene name was entirely justified.

How to change a student's view of the total situation and, hopefuly, to be able to have the student choose more socially accepted behavior responses is the process of a technique called "reframing." When applied by the teacher, this procedure helps the student view something in an event that was there all along but was unrecognized. In summary, it asks the student to look at other interpretations of the event and to choose one as a basis for future behavorial decisions.

In our case, perhaps Anne could have reframed the event by viewing it as a group prank and not as an individual one. With this perception, Anne could have said to all the girls at her lunch table: We do have fun together here with each other. I like the way we fool with each other. I guess I will have to take a little from each of you."

The Reframing Technique

Reframing is a four-step technique. In the following example, Megan, a 10-year-old LD student, is asked by the reading teacher to change her seat. Megan refuses and becomes angry.

1. *Ask the student to describe the behavior chosen that was used to respond to the event.* This first step brings the behavior into the student's consciousness. The student relives the event and the behavior response to it. If the student cannot recall, ask the student to close his or her eyes and to view the event almost like a video rebroadcast. Ask the student to recall what was heard, what was seen, and what was felt during the event.

   Megan said that the teacher asked her to move her seat to another work table. There were three boys at this table. Megan said that there was no way she was going to move. She told the teacher where to go in obscene language. She said she absolutely refused. The teacher then sent her to the office.

2. *Ask the student the purpose of the event.* The answer here will give you a key to the student's perception of the whole experience involving the disruption. You may need to be persistent with the question before you arrive at the true purpose.

   > TEACHER: What do you think the purpose of the reading teacher's request may have been?
   > MEGAN: I do not know. I hate those boys. I am not sitting with them.
   > TEACHER: What do you think the purpose was to have you sit there?
   > MEGAN: Well...she hates me...she wanted to embarrass me.

   So now the teacher has Megan's perception of the situation. Megan actually sees the reading teacher as hating her, and this one request was the teacher's way of embarrassing her.

3. *Ask the student if there are any other possible interpretations of the event.* Here you would like the student to become creative and think of other reasons why the event happened the way it did. If the student cannot think of any other perceptions, then suggest a few.

   > TEACHER: Perhaps there are other ways to look at this request.
   > MEGAN: Well, she hates me.
   > TEACHER: What other reason could she have asked you to move?
   > MEGAN: I...I don't know.
   > TEACHER: Perhaps she thinks you are mature enough, maybe even smart enough to advance to another reading station. Perhaps she thought you could handle boys.
   > MEGAN: Well...maybe.
   > TEACHER: Let's presume it is true for now. Doesn't that give a new interpretation to the event?
   > MEGAN: I guess so.

4. *Ask the student to develop three new behaviors to respond to the new interpretations.*

> TEACHER: For the moment, let's presume this is true. How differently would you have acted? What three things would you do differently?
>
> MEGAN: Well, I guess I would have gone to the table and not said anything.
>
> TEACHER: Would your feelings be different?
>
> MEGAN: I would have felt good.
>
> TEACHER: Rather than...
>
> MEGAN: Rather than angry.

If the student has difficulty generating three new behaviors, ask if he or she knows anyone in the school who would have acted differently, and ask him or her to describe the behavior.

Variations of the Reframing Technique

1. Reframing can be used to confront a disruptive student without loss of instructional time. For example, when Terry mocks Bob's answer to a teacher's question:

> BOB: I think Columbus was a strong leader.
>
> TERRY: He was an idiot!
>
> TEACHER: Say, Bobby, isn't it nice that Terry thought well enough of your answer to comment on it.

Here, the teacher, without stopping the lesson for a minute, took Terry's outburst and gave a new meaning to it. She let it be known that Terry was listening to the lesson. It is an interesting interpretation of an event we hear all too often in a classroom.

2. Reframing students' complaints can be helpful, because it gives the students a broader perspective of what is going on in the classroom. Listed are some common complaints and the teacher's reframe reference.

> STUDENT: There is too much homework in this class.
>
> TEACHER: And your grades are going up.

> STUDENT: You are too bossy.
>
> TEACHER: Yes, sometimes I do give a lot of directions. Would you wish me to ignore you?

STUDENT: She bothers me too much.
TEACHER: She likes you enough to give the very best—yourself.

HOW TO DELIVER EFFECTIVE REPRIMANDS

Reprimands are part of every teacher's daily verbal correspondence with children. A reprimand may be defined as commanding or requesting a student to stop a certain behavior that you feel is disruptive.

"Elizabeth, stop talking across the aisle."
"Jodi, sit down."

These are examples of reprimands. Of all discipline techniques used by teachers, verbal reprimands are probably the most popular. Some researchers have studied the rate of reprimands per every 15-minute period. They report that the average classroom teacher's range of reprimands is between three to five reprimands every 15 minutes. It is impossible to determine if this record is normal. A high-frequency use of reprimands, however, does not necessarily mean that the reprimands are effective. The chief question you need to ask yourself is whether your reprimand works or not. This section will help you look at your reprimand technique and decide whether or not you need to make it more effective. If you so decide, you will find a number of suggestions that you could incorporate into your own technique.

While the rate of reprimands is not important for our purposes, you may want to perform a little study of your own to determine your reprimand rate. It is suggested you have your aide or even a student, if he or she is old enough, record the number of reprimands you deliver during a 15-minute time period. Have this recording done a few times a day over a period of five days. Calculate an average rate. You could then evaluate your reprimand rate to determine if you give more reprimands in the morning or afternoon, more on Monday than on Wednesday, or more during a particular subject area than another. In any case, this self-recorded feedback will provide you with some valuable insight into your work.

The "Don't Then Do" Request

If a student is disruptive either verbally or physically, you need to intervene first to stop the disruptive behavior and then to have the student become engaged with a positive behavior. There are two types of requests here—the "don't" request and the "do" request. First, you must stop the negative behavior, and then you must start the positive. It is not easy for an angry student to move from a very negative to a very positive behavior. You first have to move him or her to a neutral position.

We cite illustrations of the three steps below:

TEACHER: Patti, stop swearing at Mike.

This is a "don't" request. The teacher is asking Patti to stop her negative behavior. Here, Patti is in a neutral position.

[Patti stops swearing.]

TEACHER: Now, Patti, pick up your pencil and copy these letters.

This is a "do" request. The teacher is asking Patti to engage in some positive behavior.

The "Don't" Request

If you have a student who has a constant annoying negative behavior, you might consider using the following procedure to extinguish this behavior.

1. *Pick* one behavior you want the student to stop. For instance:

   - Don't climb
   - Don't swear
   - Don't get out of your seat

2. *Time* the compliance to your request. If the student refrains for more than 10 seconds from the negative behavior, provide a physical reward (for younger students) or a social reward (for older students). An example of each would be a piece of cheese or candy and a statement of "good" or "excellent."

3. *Failure* to comply should result in a short discussion with the student. Tell the student your plan.

   TEACHER: [To younger student] All right, Megan, you are swearing at Michael. I will tell you not to do so the next time I hear it. If you do not swear at Michael at this time, I will give you a cookie. Do you understand?

   TEACHER: [To older student] All right, Bridie, I am trying to stop your need to swear at Michael. The next time I hear it, I will demand that you stop. If you stop, I will compliment you. You deserve to be complimented. It shows a strong will and a determination to follow directions.

You may even wish to direct some younger children to show them the right way to behave. Students who cannot remain seated and fail to comply with the teacher's request should be escorted back to their seats and shown how to sit at their desks.

Patti's Chart for Swearing

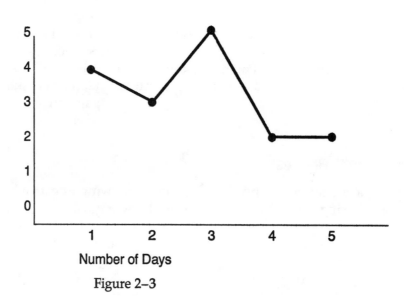

Figure 2–3

4. *Chart* the behavior to illustrate the rate of compliance to your "don't" requests. Shown in Figure 2-3 is an example of Patti's need to swear at Michael over a five-day period. By showing Patti this performance chart, you can initiate a series of discussions about why or how Patti should or can behave better during the day.

> TEACHER: Patti, the first three days you did not follow my demands to stop swearing. Looking at your chart, however, you seem to have listened more to my requests the last two days. Why the change, Patti? What is happening here?

The "Do" Request

You cannot assume that, because a student stops a negative behavior, he or she will attempt to behave positively. You may find that once you stop one negative behavior, the student assumes another negative behavior. You may need to train a student to comply with your "do" request or your request for him or her to behave positively.

In this case, follow the same procedures illustrated for the "don't" request:

1. *Pick* one behavior you would like the student to comply with.

- Do sit in your seat
- Do take out your pencil
- Do pick up the papers

2. *Time* the compliance to your request. The ten-second interval is a good measure. Reward compliance with heavy doses of praise.
3. *Failure* to comply should result in a discussion similar to the agenda shown with the don't request.
4. *Chart* the "do" behavior as you did the "don't" compliance rate.

There is one major difference between "don't" and "do" requests. When you ask a student to stop a behavior, you are actually asking that student to stop something that most likely is providing him or her with some kind of pleasure. The "do" request may or may not provide a student with pleasure, but most students will comply rather than not comply. The "don't" request is harder to comply with, because it is always harder to stop something that provides pleasure than it is to start something that might bring pleasure.

Nonverbal Support for "Do" and "Don't" Requests

There are three nonverbal behaviors that will provide you with tremendous support in attempting the "do" and the "don't" requests.

EYE CONTACT.   Always maintain direct eye contact with the student when you are talking. This may be hard to do for younger children as it will require that you bend down or sit down to reach their level. You will most likely find older students turning their heads or eyes away from you. Insist that they look at you. It's true that it makes them uncomfortable, but you are delivering a reprimand. They should feel uncomfortable. Also, if they comply with your request to look at them, your task of getting them to comply with some other behaviors will be easier. Some examples of asking a student to maintain eye contact are as follows:

"Marylou, look at me when I speak with you."
"Helen, I can't see your eyes."
"Anthony, could you look at me? Thank you."

PROXIMITY.   A reprimand needs to be delivered from a close distance. A good rule of thumb is to stand a minimum of two feet or a maximum of three feet away from the student. If you stand too close, within two feet, you may seem physically threatening to the student. Our culture does not accept a close physical contact when talking or dialoguing. On the other hand, if you stand more than three feet away, you lose some of your effectiveness. Eye contact is not as direct, and your physical confrontation is weakened. Remember, you want to support your verbal requests with a strong physical presence.

Touch is also important. If the student is not too threatened by the act, it is proper to touch the student lightly on the shoulder as you deliver the reprimand. To do this, you move in closer than the two feet minimum distance, touch lightly, and then return to your original position. The kinesthetic feeling of your touch will help ground or solidify your verbal requests.

VOICE.   The intensity of your voice need not be high to deliver an effective reprimand. It is best that you maintain your original vocal intensity when requesting. You want the student to hear your words, not concentrate on the loudness, tenseness, or anger in your voice. Pause three to four seconds after you speak, maintaining your direct eye contact and your proximity to the student. Allow the message to "sink in."

Group Reprimand

You may find that many students in your class exhibit the same negative behavior. It may be necessary to reprimand one student publicly in order to deliver the message to all students. For example, when a student comes late to class, you may want to deliver a public reprimand if there are others in the room who also come late often.

TEACHER: [Stops teaching and moves over within three feet of Marylou, a 14-year-old who arrives late to class] Marylou, where have you been?

MARYLOU: I had to see somebody.

TEACHER: Do you have a pass?

MARYLOU: No [turns her eyes down].

TEACHER: Marylou, look at me when I speak. Thank you. Now you are late. Do not be late again, or you will be detained after school. Do you understand? [This is a "don't" request.]

MARYLOU: Yes.

TEACHER: Okay, get your social studies book and open to page 31. The class and I will wait for you. [This is a "do" request.]

You can also deliver reprimands nonverbally. If you find that wearing coats or hats or carrying radios is a constant problem, you simply take one student's illicit object and hold it in your hand for a while for all to see. Let others see that you confiscate these items. The message will get out to students not to bring them or else have them taken. One principal will make a point of taking a forbidden radio away from a student and carrying it through the school cafeteria for all to see. Every student is reminded that radios will be confiscated. It is a powerful message.

HOW TO USE VERBAL MESSAGES TO CONTROL NONVERBAL BEHAVIOR

This technique is geared toward retarded students. It probably will not work well with students who are classified as other than EMR or TMR.

There is a very complex relationship between verbal and nonverbal behavior. There is research to show that verbal statements can control nonverbal behavior and that nonverbal behavior can control verbal statements. This procedure will demonstate how you can use verbal statements to train a retarded student to comply with nonverbal behavior. This procedure works very well if you wish to teach a student to share, praise, remain in seat, or remain on-task with greater frequency.

A Four-Step Procedure

You must first determine which behavior you would like the student to manifest more frequently. Define this behvior fairly specifically. For example, you would like Ginny to sit at her desk more during the class. Or, you might like Katie to share her toys more with the other students. Once this behavior is decided on, you can begin the student's training.

STEP 1.   On the first day of training, ask the student a very specific question. For example,

"Ginny, are you going to stay in your seat today?"
"Katie, will you share your toys today?"

Repeat this request every day for three days.

STEP 2.   On the fourth day ask the student if he/she knows what behavior you are talking about. No matter what the response of the student may be, explain exactly what you mean.

"Ginny, what I mean by remaining in your seat is that your buttocks be in the seat, and your two feet be on the floor."
"Katie, by sharing your toys, I am asking you to sit next to one other girl, and for the two of you to play with your toy."

You may even have to demonstrate or show the student how to do this behavior. Lead him or her through the vairous steps to maintain this behavior. Now, ask the student if he or she is going to comply with your request.

STEP 3.   At the end of the fourth-day class period, make one of the following statements to the student:

"Ginny, you said you would remain in your seat, and you did. You did great."

"Ginny, you said you would remain in your seat, and you did not."

If the student did comply with your request, you could reward the student with candy or popcorn. Take the student outside for a walk or allow him or her to read a favorite magazine or play with a favorite toy as other examples of reward.

If the student failed to comply, you should describe the behavior you are requesting once again as you did in Step 3. Make a statement, such as the following:

"Okay, Ginny, you did not remain in your seat the entire period as I requested. I would like you to try harder. I know you could do better at it. Let's try again tomorrow."

STEP 4.   For the next five days, continue the same procedure; that is, ask the student if he or she is going to comply with your request. Observe the student to determine the appropriate behavior. If the student complies, follow up with the predetermined reward. If the student fails to comply, then repeat the request and demonstrate the behavior.

If you have five straight days of compliance, you will be able to withdraw the reward system. You will find that the change in behavior will be maintained. If the student starts to slip and not comply on a consistent basis, then reinstitute the reward system but on an every-other-day basis.

If the student cannot maintain five perfect days of compliance, change the behavior you are requesting the student to change. Pick a less difficult behavior to begin with. Gradually, increase your demands until the original behavior you are seeking is demonstrated by the student. For example, if Katie cannot comply with your request that she share her toys, you might spend the first two-week period asking her to sit next to another student. After two weeks of compliance with this request, ask her to share her toys with the student.

Charting the Behavior

When you first start out with this procedure with a student, you may wish to rate the behavior you wish to extinguish or reduce. This will give you a baseline to judge whether or not progress is being made. Once you begin the verbal requests, count to see if the student is displaying a certain behavior less than before. You probably will not be able to reduce the occurrence of a disruptive behavior to zero within five days, but you will reduce it significantly. Once the reduction process sets in, you will have to determine how frequently you can tolerate the specific disruptive behavior. For example, Ginny's teacher was able to reduce her out-of-seat behavior from 10 times per 50 minutes to three times per 50 minutes. For the teacher, that rate was quite acceptable.

HOW TO DEAL WITH STUDENT
VERBAL RESISTANCE TO CHANGE .

Some students are excellent resisters. They invest an enormous amount of energy and time in their attempts to avoid the behavorial change you are requesting of them. In this chapter, a number of verbal behavorial change techniques are described. What if a student resists you when you implement one of these techniques? Usually, the resistance will come in a verbal form. This section will describe a number of ways a student may verbally resist you, and other ways to deal with this resistance.

The five types of verbal resistance described here are based on an article, "Observation of Client Resistance," by Patricia Chamberlain, Gerald Patterson, John Reid, Kathryn Kavanagh, and Marion Forgatch (*Behavior Therapy, 15,* 1984: 144-155). A brief dialogue will introduce each type to illustrate its use, which is followed by an explanation of the process. The verbal techniques used to deal with these resistances are also listed, together with examples on how to apply them.

In general, there are three types of responses a teacher can use. In the *interpretation* response, the teacher actually tells the student the type of verbal resistance he or she is using. When used, this response helps the student become aware of what he or she is doing and also tends to elicit a discussion on the student's attempts to resist.

The *assertive* response is a little more declarative. It informs the student that verbal resistance will not be tolerated and that student discussion focusing on such resistance will be ignored.

The third type of response is that of a *question* type. This response tends to open the discussion between the teacher and the student to other aspects of the student's behavior. The presenting behavior problem is set aside for a time, and the teacher and student discuss the student's need to resist.

1. *The Confronting Resistance*

TEACHER: Now, Richard, you are ten minutes late to my class.
RICHARD: I am not. You don't know when I left. I really am only five minutes late. You said once I could be five minutes late if I was coming from gym.
TEACHER: I was sure I saw you leave.
RICHARD: It could not have been me!

This is a confronting resistance because the student is challenging the teacher's judgment and perhaps even her authority. Possible responses to this type of resistance are noted.

INTERPRETATION Richard, you are confronting me on this issue.
ASSERTIVE Richard, do not tell me what I know or do not know. I saw you come in ten minutes late. We are not discussing my judgment.

QUESTION Why do you question my judgment here, Richard?

2. *The Talkover Resistance*

TEACHER: Now, Regina, I asked you to finish...
REGINA: I have.
TEACHER: Not your lunch.
REGINA: Please, I am talking now.

It is difficult in print to characterize this resistance, because the student quite literally talks over the teacher or interrupts the teacher. You will find yourself in this situation if you discover your sentences half-completed. Possible responses to this type of resistance are noted.

INTERPRETATION Regina, you are talking over me.
ASSERTIVE Regina, let me finish my sentences.
QUESTION Why do I feel that I can't finish my sentences with you?

3. *The Avoidance Resistance*

TEACHER: Marylou, how about sitting down now and doing some work?
MARYLOU: Huh?
TEACHER: Please sit down.
MARYLOU: I am going to see Timmy. I have to ask him something.

Using this resistance, the student can effectively block the teacher's attempt to change behavior, because new topics are introduced that lead the teacher off the topic. After a few minutes in this type of dialogue resistance, the teacher may wonder how the discussion ever got on this or that topic or, worse, how to get out of it. Here are some techniques to use to get back on the track.

INTERPRETATION Marylou, you are talking about something I am not talking about.
ASSERTIVE Marylou, let's stay on the topic I am talking about.
QUESTION Why do you continually change the topic, Marylou?

4. *The Negative Resistance*

TEACHER: I asked you to complete ten problems for homework, Tim.

TIM: I couldn't do them all. You know I had to cover the game yesterday afternoon. There was no time.

TEACHER: Game or no game, you had ten problems to do last night.

TIM: It was just impossible to do.

Blaming others, statements of hopelessness, defeat and depression are what you will find with this type of resistance. The student is so negative and defeatist that the teacher will feel the resistance like a brick wall. To penetrate these defenses, try one of these techniques:

INTERPRETATION Tim, once again, you are so negative with this issue.

ASSERTIVE Stop blaming others and take some responsibility for this.

QUESTION Why blame others for this failure, Tim?

5. *The Inattention Resistance*

TEACHER: Helen, Evelyn said you hit her during lunch.

HELEN: She never said that.

TEACHER: Oh yes, and, furthermore, she said you would get her if she told me.

HELEN: [Looking across the room at two students talking]

TEACHER: Helen, are you listening to me?

With this resistance the student loses focus with the teacher and seems to be preoccupied with something else. In effect, the teacher has to gain the student's attention again before the verbal dialogue can continue.

INTERPRETATION Helen, you are avoiding the question.

ASSERTIVE Pay attention to what I am saying, Helen.

QUESTION Why can't you pay attention to what I am saying?

CHAPTER 2 REFERENCES

Bandler, Richard, and John Grinder. *Reframing.* Moab, UT: Real People Press, 1982.

Beck, Aaron. *Cognitive Therapy and the Emotional Disorders.* New York: Meridian Books, 1976.

Chamberlain, Patricia, Gerald Patterson, John Reid, Kathryn Kavanagh, and Martin Forgatch. "Observation of Client Resistance." *Behavior Therapy, 15,* 1984, 144-155.

Davis, K.L., MA. Hector, N. Meara, J. King, D. Tracy, and J. Wyeoff. "Teaching Counselor Trainees to Respond Consistently to Different Aspects of Anger." *Journal of Counseling Psychology, 32,* 1985, 580-588.

Fassler, Joan. *Helping Children Cope: Mastering Stress Through Books and Their Stories.* New York: Free Press, 1978.

Kendall, P.C., and S. D. Hallon (eds.). *Cognitive-Behavioral Interventions: Theory, Research, and Procedures.* New York: Academic Press, 1979.

Lindeman, Barbara, and Martin Kling. "Bibliotherapy: Definitions, Uses, Studies." *Journal of School Psychology, 2,* 1969, 36-41.

Mahoney, Michael. *Cognition and Behavior Modification.* Cambridge, MA: Ballinger Publishing, 1974.

Mahoney, Michael J., and Carl E. Thoresen. *Self Control: Power to the Person.* Monterey, CA: Brooks/Coles Publishing, 1974.

chapter 3
_____

WORKING EFFECTIVELY
WITH PARENTS

As teachers of special education children, we are required by law to involve parents in the educational planning for their children. Parents can be a great source of strength and help to teachers during the course of a school year. Teachers need to learn how to work with parents toward the common goal of improving the child. As a teacher, you will find a full range of parental involvement in school affairs. There will be parents who question everything you do, parents who cooperate fully, and parents who show little concern for what you do. You are required to work with parents such as these and with many other types of parents. In this chapter are a number of ideas you will find helpful to use during parent conferences. Some of the ideas are to be used for specific occasions; others are general in nature, and these you can adapt to meet your own specific needs. However you use them, you will find that they will dramatically increase your knowledge and operation skills in working effectively with parents.

HOW TO UNDERSTAND THE ROLES FAMILY MEMBERS PLAY DURING A CONFERENCE

One of every special educator's responsibilities is the need to meet with the parents and/or guardians of the students. Some of these meetings are for the purpose of reviewing the annual individualized education plan (IEP), behavior problems, mid-semester reports, and/or parent education workshops. For each of these conferences, a teacher usually has at least a mother or female guardian present and, quite often, other family members as well. Most teachers are neither trained to understand nor deal with the interactions that take place during a parent/teacher conference. It is the purpose of this section to present the teacher with a comprehensive view of typical operating roles of family members and suggestions a teacher may use to facilitate conference interaction.

When examining the roles families act out, you should remember that, although only one or two members of a family may be present at a conference, there may be other family members not present who occupy certain roles in the family. By understanding all the roles a family may play, whether or not all family members are actually present, the teacher will be more effective in facilitating change.

According to Virginia Satir, there are four roles family members may occupy. (This section is adapted by permission of the author and publisher, Virginia Satir, *Conjoint Family Therapy*, Palo Alto, CA: Science & Behavior Books, Inc., Rev. Expanded, 1983):

1. The Placator
2. The Blamer
3. The Computer
4. The Distractor

These roles are evident when a family unit is under stress. Usually, a parent/teacher conference is a stressful situation for a family unit even when positive things are being reported. Stress is defined here as an emotional tension that causes body or mental pain and/or anxiety. Most teachers, when they read through these roles, will easily recognize the behavior not only in the families of their students but also in the behavior of their own family. This section could serve as an interesting self-study. Below are listed the four roles and some suggested ways to deal with each.

The Placator

This person tries to make everyone happy, often to the point of denying him- or herself. Typically, one would view this person as a peacemaker. He or she speaks in low tones, generally avoids eye contact, and does not express him- or herself in physical terms. He or she likes to talk, to discuss, and to reach a compromise among family members rather than let anger exist in the family. He or she expresses a lot of magical thinking, always hoping that things will and can get better, even without changing anything. For this reason, he or she tends to be future-oriented. He or she avoids the painful feelings that exist in a family unit at the moment and denies the past bad experiences.

An example of a family member playing a placator role follows:

TEACHER: Now, Terry has to improve. He is too lazy and does not work hard.

MOTHER: Oh, yes, I promise you will have no problems with him. He will start working as of this moment.

TEACHER: But you must understand. He is behind in everything. He says he wants to be a doctor. He will never make it. He cannot do his classwork now.

MOTHER: Oh, things cannot be that bad. I am sure that, if you look closely, you will find him doing what you ask. He is so smart that he will probably even marry a doctor.

One can see the future orientation in this mother's dialogue, as well as the need to smooth over the teacher's feelings that Terry is not working. The role of a placator is clear here.

Suggestions for interaction are as follows:

- Keep these individuals from talking too much.
- Ask them to be specific.
- Be assertive in interrupting them and demanding that they look at you.
- Protect them from other family members who might want to blame them for things that have gone wrong.
- Keep them focused on the present situation.

The Blamer

People who occupy this role tend to accuse others in the family of having caused or perpetuated the problem. They will blame everyone including the teacher, the superintendent, and the school for the behavior of a child rather than focus on what might be the real problem. They often become very angry toward the child, and they shift the blame for many of the family's shortcomings to a family member rather than deal with the responsibility. These individuals are usually loud, interrupt others, point their finger at others, become excited, and give orders to others in the family.

An example of a blamer role is as follows:

TEACHER: Now, Tommy needs to work harder at his math if he wishes to move to seventh-grade work next year.

FATHER: Tommy is not the problem. If his mother would just stop babying him! She should let him grow up and let him make mistakes. He will learn from experiences.

TEACHER: But what about the math?

FATHER: Aw, he won't need that stuff. Teach him how to use a calculator.

TEACHER: Well, yesterday he got...

FATHER: I don't care about yesterday. You and his mother need to talk about this. His mother. Now *there* is the problem.

Suggestions for interaction are as follows:

- Ask them specific questions with lead words, such as "how," "when," "where," or "why."
- Avoid allowing these individuals to take the leadership role from you by their excessive talking.
- Challenge all generalizations, such as "all," "everyone," "we."
- Ask them what they do when they get angry.
- Refocus their anger from the child to that of family rules, regulations, and how members interact.
- Ask them to calm down and to avoid finger pointing.

The Computer

One envisions a computer as a mechanical device that can produce a lot of data but no feelings. Such is the image of a person who occupies the position of a computer in the family. This individual seems unaffected by the emotional ups-and-downs that are part of every family's interactions. They speak and respond to other family members and will even initiate conversations. They sound reasonable and intelligent, but they speak with little conviction. They generally avoid active interaction during a conference. Their body positions are usually rigid, and they rarely maintain eye contact with the other family members.

An example of a computer role is as follows:

TEACHER: What do you think of the situation, Stan?
STAN: It sounds like it has merit.
TEACHER: Do you feel your son can do it?
STAN: He has the potential.
TEACHER: Do you foresee any problems?
STAN: Not at this moment.

In this case, it is apparent that Stan is only going to respond with the minimum amount of information requested. It may also appear that he is committing his thoughts or feelings to the proposed situation. While sounding committed, he is, in fact, uncommitted.

Suggestions for interaction are as follows:

- Make him or her say "I" before a statement. "*I* think so," "*I* feel good about it," "*I* am happy" are statements of commitment.
- Ask him or her what he or she thinks or feels about what another family member may have just said.
- Ask him or her not to evaluate another's behavior or feelings by guessing what the intent of that person's behavior may be.

The Distractor

Individuals who play this role tend to disrupt the conference. They do this either by acting out or by passively avoiding the interaction. They make jokes during a conference, answer questions with questions, try to change the subject, and even try to engage in a private conversation with another family member. They tend to be restless during a conversation and will touch things and others, often to distract. They might even move around the room and engage in quasi-meaningless activities.

An example of a distractor role is as follows:

TEACHER: [To the parents] You could try to get a physical for your son before we try other assessments.

TOMMY: You think I'm sick... Hey, Lynn [his sister], how about we go get some ice cream before I croak! [He laughs]

PARENTS: Now, Tommy, you sit right there.

TOMMY: I'm afraid to leave. I may drop dead here.

Tommy is making a joke of the teacher's recommendation that he get a physical. He attempts to engage his sister in a private, yet distracting, conversation. You can see it worked because, at the end of this scenario, he has even pulled his parents into his private joke.

Suggestions for interaction are as follows:

● When he or she does start to distract, move over and sit next to him or her.

● When he or she starts to become distractive, simply touch him or her or take his or her play object away.

● If he or she answers your question with a question, inform him or her of that behavior.

● Try asking him or her to answer a question you pose in his or her mind silently.

● Watch that the family member who occupies the blamer role does not unleash a lot of anger upon this individual.

A Sample Family Conference

Figure 3-1 is a typical conference called by a teacher to discuss John's apparent lack of progress in school. John, his mother, his stepfather, and his two sisters, Marylou and Ginny, attended the conference. John is a retarded 19-year-old; his two sisters are normal-developed 14- and 13-year-olds. In the figure, you will note that comments are made alongside the dialogue to indicate when a particular family role is occupied. Note the successful responses of the teacher to deal with the dynamics of this conference.

TEACHER:	I have asked you here today to discuss John's lack of progress this year.	[Conference object is stated up front as a reminder of the task]
MOTHER:	Well, yes, I must say we did not all have to come. I am sure a meeting between you and me could solve this problem. After all, I am willing to try anything to get John back on-task.	[Placator role]
STEPFATHER:	Yeah, this is an issue for the teacher. If you do your job, there will be no telling what progress John could make. He may be retarded, but if you taught him right, he could learn. Although, I admit he is dumb a bit.	[Blamer role]
TEACHER:	I am not trying to lay blame on anyone for his lack of progress. I would like us to work together to help him accomplish a few tasks.	
GINNY:	[Starts to take her watch off and look at the dial, then holds it to her ear] Hey, John, listen to this tick.	[Distractor role]
JOHN:	[Takes watch] Yeah, listen.	
MARYLOU:	Now let's pay attention and get on with the things the teacher would like us to talk about.	[Computer role]
TEACHER:	Ginny, may I hold that watch during our meeting. It is a bit distracting.	[The teacher is attempting to neutralize the distractor]
STEPFATHER:	Hey, kids, pay attention. You are causing too much noise.	[The blamer attacks the distractor and the computer]
TEACHER:	As I said, I wonder if it is possible for us to make a plan to deal with John's need to improve his school work.	

Figure 3–1

STEPFATHER:	We have tried. Nothing works.	[The blamer generalizes with the use of "we" and "nothing"]
TEACHER:	You mean everyone in the family has tried, and absolutely nothing has worked?	[Here the teacher challenges the blamer]
MOTHER:	He doesn't mean it that way. I remember two years ago with another teacher... You remember her, John. What's her name?... Things were better then. I wish...	[The mother tries to placate the stepfather's role. Then she rambles on about the past]
TEACHER:	Well, I am sure it was. However, this year John is not doing enough. Can we plan some home activities for him that involve the whole family?	

Figure 3—1 (continued)

By the end of the sample conference, you can see that the teacher is active in the first few minutes of this conference in trying to keep the various family members focused on the task. This teacher successfully used various strategies discussed earlier with each of the different manifest roles to keep charge of this parent conference.

HOW TO GIVE PARENTS ADVICE

Often, the special education teacher is called on to participate in parent workshops or to provide advice to parents who have serious questions about the appropriate manner to raise their children. The teacher is viewed as an expert in both educational tactics and behavioral management techniques. Parents often use the teacher as the first source of advice. The answers a teacher provides should not only assist the parent but also establish the teacher as a credible authority in some areas of child-rearing. While very often the advice a teacher must give is child-specific—that is, geared to the specific needs of a specific child—more often than not the advice can be in a generalized format. In these cases, it is the task of the parent to apply this advice to his or her specific needs.

It is the purpose of this section to provide the teacher with general advice-giving ideas. These ideas are divided into academic areas and behavior management areas for the purpose of organization. Often, as any teacher knows, the two areas are interrelated and mutually dependent. For the purposes of clarity, however, they are outlined as two separate areas. You will find that a discussion of each idea will provide you with some background information. This information will provide you with a greater in-depth understanding of how to implement the idea.

Academic Advice for Parents

1. ORGANIZE THE CHILD'S STUDY TIME.   Students need help in establishing home-study time. This is true whether the child is six or sixteen. It is wise to outline a set pattern of study with parents that clearly establishes what needs to be studied, where it will be studied, when it will be studied, and even how it will be studied.

When the child comes home from school, have the parent discuss with the child what the homework assignment is for the night. The parent should not assume there is no homework. Establish a phone-buddy system in which the child can call a classmate if, by chance, the assignment is forgotten, lost, or denied. Have the parent post the assignment on the refrigerator door or on some other dominant place of view at home.

The parent should establish a time each night when homework will be done. To avoid the constant reminding of time that a parent can find him- or herself in, make this time contingent on some other structured event. For example, study time at some homes begins immediately after dinner, or immediately after a particular favorite television show, or when the child comes home from Little League.

The place of study is important. The parent should never have the child do homework in a room where other activity is more attractive. Younger children will like to do their work in the vicinity of an adult. In this case, make sure the television set is off, running or active game-playing by siblings is over, and that even distracting things like eating dessert is over. For older children, a bedroom or other quiet place is appropriate. During study time, phone calls and other disruptions should be eliminated. Parents should discourage the child from studying in bed or with a radio on. When the study is completed, the parent should review what has been done. Some teachers require a parent signature on the work. In any case, the parent should check to see if it has been done and, if possible, whether it has been done correctly. The parent and student talk about the work in a general way. *Remember:* If the parent shows an interest in the work, the child will show an interest.

The "how" of study is also important. Homework can take many forms: it can be a writing or reading assignment, studying for a test, watching an assigned television show, or even doing work on a long-range project. Most teachers warn students of tests, so a parent can help the child by dividing the material to be studied into smaller units, with a night to study each unit. Use one night, usually the night before, to review for the test. If there is a research project to be done, a parent should make a long-term schedule of what needs to be done. In these cases, the parent should post the schedule and then each day cross off the particular task that has been done with the child.

Some teachers do not give homework on weekends. The parent may want to keep to the study time even for Friday nights. This night could be for reviewing the week's work, writing a letter to a relative, or for reading a few pages in a book. The parent can increase home-study time by 20 percent if the child studies on Friday nights.

2. MONITOR THE CHILD'S TIME.   The younger the child, the more his or her time needs to be monitored and structured. In addition to set study time, TV-watching time needs to be restricted. Children just do not need to have the television set on every hour they are home. The parent should decide which programs the child can watch and then turn off the set. The time to come in from playing outside also needs to be set. The parent should stick to the rules on the time, but be flexible on occasions if a special event occurs. The time for bed also needs to be established. Elementary-school children need to be in bed between 8:00 and 9:00 p.m. Secondary school children may have their hours extended to 10:00 or 10:30 p.m. Whether a child goes to sleep or not is not critical, but it is important that school children be in their beds ready for sleep at the appointed hour. They can quietly play, listen to the radio, or read before sleep if they wish; it is important to establish a "quiet time." Interestingly, many parents report that it is more important to establish bedtime for younger children than it is to establish a time for them to come in from the outside. For some reason, younger children come into the house easily enough but will try to extend their awake hours as long as possible. For older children, the reverse happens. It is easier to get them to bed than it is to get them to come home on time. If the child works after school, the parent should be sure that the work hours are not too extensive. If fatigue, lack of social time, or poor grades result, then work hours need to be cut. The parent should call the school if the child's employer is not flexible.

3. KEEP STUDY AIDS AT HOME.   The parent can help the child study by providing materials for the child to use. A dictionary, a map of the state and the nation, and even an encyclopedia set will be a great resource for the child. Even more basic is the need for pens, pencils, paper, and rulers. These should be kept in a box or old coffee can and be used only for study-related activities. These aids make excellent birthday and holiday gifts. By giving such presents, the parent is telling the child how important study is in the home.

4. TALK ABOUT SCHOOL.   The parent should show an interest in the child's work. Dinner time is an excellent time for the parent to ask about what happened in school. The parent should not accept the comment, "Aw, nothing." Something is always happening in class. The parent should applaud the child's achievements, and post good papers brought home, good report cards, and other records of accomplishment. The parent should be careful not to scold poor achievement. It is best to ask a child why he or she thinks a particular assignment was done poorly. The parent should probe the reasons why a mistake was made and help the child plan alternative ways to avoid making the same mistakes.

It is easy for a parent to make ordinary at-home experiences interesting learning experiences. If the parent and child are watching television, the parent could ask the child questions to make him or her think. For example:

- What happened here?
- What was that character thinking and feeling?
- How would you change the ending?
- Did you study that issue in school?

Another strategy, especially for older children, is for the parent and child to watch the news together. During the commercials, they can talk about what has been viewed. This need not be done every night; rather, choose two or three times a week to share the news together.

The parent can also use a child's dictionary to pick a "word for the day" to learn. Have the parent post the word in a dominant place at home. Then, the child should use the word in sentences and note every time he or she hears it used that day.

The parent can always ask you for home-related learning activities that are fun and study-relate.

Form 3-1 summarizes these study tips for parents. You might want to make copies of the sheet and give a copy to each parent in your class.

Behavior Advice for Parents

1. SET AS FEW RULES AS POSSIBLE; THEN STICK TO THEM.   The more rules the parent has, the more work he or she will have in enforcing them. The parent should decide which rules are the most needed and sit down with the child and discuss them. For younger children, the parent should inform the child of the rules. For older, more mature students, the parent should hold a less formal discussion. The parent should explain why such-and-such a rule is needed and what he or she expects from the child. The point to remember in establishing rules is to allow the child to feel that he or she knows why the parent needs a rule. The parent is the boss, however, and his or her rules are not open for change.

The parent should expect the rules to be tested. Every child tests rules; it is part of growing up. Avoid nagging the child about rules; a reminder or two is all that is necessary. If compliance does not occur, then the parent should implement consequences for not following rules. These consequences should be natural ones that are logically connected to the broken rules. For example, if an 11-year-old comes home after curfew, the parent should take away his or her privilege to go out for the next few nights. Taking away dessert for a night or two may be punishing, but it is not logically connected to the offense.

2. LISTEN TO THE CHILD.   Listening takes work. In a parent's busy schedule, listening often needs to take a back seat. When it comes to certain issues,

A PARENT'S GUIDE TO STUDY TIPS

Organize Your Child's Study Time
Set a pattern of study that clearly establishes what needs to be studied, where it will be studied, when it will be studied, and how it will be studied.

Monitor Your Child's Time
The younger the child, the more structure is needed. Study, curfew, and bedtime should be clearly known to both child and parent.

Keep Study Aids at Home
Give educational items, pens, pencils, papers, rulers, dictionaries, and maps as presents at birthdays. Make opportunities at home learning opportunities.

Talk about School
If you show an interest, your children will show an interest.

Form 3-1

however, the parent needs to listen. The parent should remind him- or herself daily that listening is work. Here are few tips to good listening. Make eye contact with the child; relate back to the child the facts of what he or she said; try to picture what happened or the circumstances of the situation; avoid judging the action; summarize what the child said and, if asked for, give his or her feelings about the situation. If the parent is in doubt, he or she should ask the child if an opinion is wanted.

3. TALK TO THE CHILD.   There are times to listen and times to talk. While all parents talk to their children, there are a few hints that can make the talking a more two-sided communication. The first hint is to avoid preaching. Children will test a parent's standards and rules. They say things that will surprise parents. The easiest thing to do, in return, is to preach about what is good and bad; that is, repeating the message over and over again. Instead, say it once, and be done with it.

Another hint is to avoid zapping or killer statements. These are name-calling statements that only antagonize the child. Parent should let the child finish speaking before responding. The parent should not interrupt. The parent should own his or her own problems by stating things with the word, "I." For example, "I am upset at you," or, "I am confused," rather than saying, "This is upsetting," or, "This issue is confusing." The parent should also stick to the topic being discussed. It is easy to bring up other issues when discussing a particular topic. The parent should avoid cross-complaining; that is, responding to a complaint from the child by complaining about him or her.

Finally, if the parent feels he or she is getting angry about an issue, tell the child. The parent should withdraw from the conversation and return to it at a later date.

4. MAINTAIN THE GENERATION GAP.   Children need their parents as "Parents." They do not need parents as other friends. When the parent relates with the child, it should be as a parent. That means that the parent should express his or her ideas, values, and opinions even if they conflict with those of the child. The parent should avoid seeking personal advice from the child. Children have their own growing pains and identity crises; they do not need to take on those of their parents.

The parent should not make promises he or she cannot keep. If, for some unpredictable reason, a promise must be broken, the parent should explain it to the child in a way that she or he understands. Then make it up to the child as soon as possible.

The parent should always accept the child as special, no matter what the child may do or say as he or she grows up. The child will hurt, insult, frustrate, and cause the parent all kinds of grief as he or she grows up. The key to a parent's maintaining sanity during these times is to remind him- or herself that these actions are not malicious. They are a normal part of a parent/child relationship.

5. TELL THE CHILD THAT HE OR SHE IS SPECIAL.   Always and in as many ways as possible, the parent should tell the child that he or she is loved and respected. There are many formal symbolic rituals to tell children they are special. Birthdays, graduations, plays, and various religious events are some examples. Children, however, need more special attention. The parent should applaud the child when he or she comes home with good school papers. The parent should post the papers and make a fuss about them. If the parent does this when the child is six years old, the child will not only expect it but want the fuss when he or she is sixteen. There is probably no greater way to say the child is special than spending time with him or her.

Form 3-2 summarizes these behavior tips for parents. You might want to make copies of the sheet and give a copy to each parent in your class.

HOW TO CONDUCT A SUCCESSFUL IEP CONFERENCE

As a special education teacher, you are required by law to hold conferences with parents for the purpose of determining the child's needs, what services will be provided to meet these needs, and what you expect the outcome will be (*Federal Register*, 1981, page 5462).

It is clear that the intent of the law is to provide parents with "equal" participation in the educational decisions of the child. As a teacher, you know that parental involvement in IEP conferences varies considerably. Some parents are involved in every major decision; some question your recommendations; some want their own decisions implemented; some do not care; some never show up for conferences; and there are some parents who do not understand what the whole process is all about. Working with parents at IEP conferences takes some skills. These skills are not necessarily the same as those needed to be an excellent teacher of a special-education classroom. Therefore, it is the purpose of this section to provide the reader with a few skills that might be helpful in working with parents during an IEP conference.

Teacher Expectations

You will need to examine your own expectations about parent involvement in IEP conferences. Very often, a teacher will judge a parent's total involvement with a child based on his or her educational involvement with his or her child. For some teachers, if a parent comes to the IEP conferences, agrees to the objectives outlined, and signs consent, he or she is judged as "involved." Whereas, parents who do not show up for conferences are judged as being "uninvolved." There is an obvious flaw in this judging process, because the teacher is basing his or her judgment of the parent solely on whether the parent conforms to expectations of proper behavior at IEP conferences.

A PARENT'S GUIDE TO BEHAVIOR TIPS

Set as Few Rules as Possible; Then Stick to Them
Rules should be clear, few in number, and they should be explained to your children. Expect them to be tested. Do not punish, but let natural consequences occur if a rule is broken.

Listen to Your Child
Listening takes work. Some issues need to be heard by you. Give your attention and summarize what your child has said.

Talk to Your Child
There are times your child needs to hear your opinion. Do not preach it, but explain it so that your children may understand your view. They may or may not accept your view, but, at least, they will understand you.

Maintain the Generation Gap
Your children need you as parents, not as friends. Your lifestyle is appropriate for you, and their style, for them. They do not expect you to be like them, but to like them.

Tell Your Children They Are Special
In many ways, always convey to your children that they are unique and special, and that you love and respect them. If you do, they will feel the same toward you.

© 1988 by The Center for Applied Research in Education

Form 3-2

There are many parents who, for many reasons, are not educationally involved with their child, but who nonetheless are very parentally involved with them. These parents choose not to become involved in the schools for their own reasons, yet they are very good parents.

So, as a teacher of special education students, you need to look at your own expectations of parental involvement. Figure 3-2 lists a few questions for you to consider.

If you answered "yes" to all of these questions, then perhaps it might be a good idea for you to examine your expectations of parents. Generally speaking, there are few parents capable of living up to all these expectations. Yet, it is easy for a teacher to judge a parent who fails in one or more of these categories as being a "bad" or "uninvolved" parent. A suggestion to any teacher of a handicapped child is to judge each parent on his or her own particular preference of involvement with the school. Parents, like their children, are seeking to adjust themselves to the legal-educational-psychological jargon of special education. For *their* own good, not the teacher's, they may seek to avoid or alter parts of this involvement.

Parent Expectations

A teacher also needs to determine the expectations of the parents. These expectations can range from believing the teacher can do all things to believing he or she can do very little. Parent expectations involve their level of trust in the teacher. These expectations are easily viewed at IEP conferences, as is the level of trust they have in the teacher. A measure of parental expectations can be obtained in two—in some cases three—different ways. Figure 3-3 shows each of these ways together with a range chart you can use to assess in advance where you feel the parents' expectations are.

		Yes	No
1.	Do you expect to attend all the school conferences?	_____	_____
2.	Do you expect parents to agree with all your recommendations?	_____	_____
3.	Do you expect parents to participate in their child's school program?	_____	_____
4.	Do you expect parents to come during the day for conferences?	_____	_____
5.	Do you expect parents to understand everything you say?	_____	_____

Figure 3–2

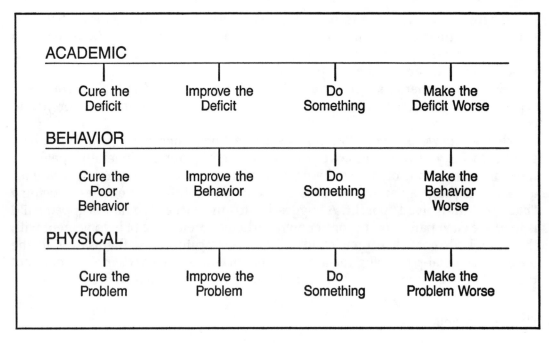

Figure 3–3

Conference Situation

The teacher should look at his or her expectations and the projected expectations of the parents and make some decisions regarding the outcome of the IEP conference. The teacher needs to ask the questions given in Form 3-3.

Conference Skills

Below are a number of suggested skills a teacher should use during an IEP conference. These skills will make the mutually agreeable expectations easier to facilitate and make those potential areas of disagreement clearer and possibly resolvable.

AVOID TECHNICAL TERMS.   Very often, parents become perplexed when educational jargon is used that is not part of the normal vocabulary used in education. This overuse of jargon can occur especially if the teacher adheres to a particular theoretical treatment program. Very often, advocates of such programs use program jargon to sum up or join together pieces of behavior that are evident in a child. For example, if a teacher believes in the psychoanalytic model, then the use of a term, such as "id," would mean a lot to this teacher but, most likely, not very much to the parents. No matter what school of thought you follow, it becomes most clear and provides more information to parents if you can describe the various terms you use in layperson's terms.

Name of Student_____ Grade_____

TEACHER'S EXPECTATIONS OF IEP CONFERENCE

1. What do I want to accomplish at this conference? (List them here.)

_____

_____

_____

_____

2. What do the parents want to accomplish at this conference? (List them here.)

_____

_____

_____

_____

3. Are these areas of mutual agreement? (List them here.)

_____

_____

_____

_____

4. Are there areas of disagreement? (List them here.)

_____

_____

_____

_____

Form 3-3

AVOID INTERPRETING TEST DATA AS JUST DATA.   As with the problem of technical jargon, there is often confusion about how to interpret test data. Most parents do not know a WISC-R from a TAT test, so using data and terms from a particular test can be confusing. Take, for example, a paragraph used in a local testing situation as read to parents at a conference.

> This norm grade applies to the PR-S and NCE. It also applies to the subtest and cluster performance rating when your child was tested within the grade range for which norms are available.

To most parents, this statement means absolutely nothing. What the parents need to know is whether their child is reading at grade level or not.

DESCRIBE CHILD'S BEHAVIOR SPECIFICALLY.   Parents want to know what the teacher sees about their child as being at developmental grade level, and that which needs remedial work. They are relying on the teacher's experience to make comparative judgments. For example, a teacher may describe the social adjustment of a second-grade learning-disabled boy with these descriptive words:

- Dennis has close friends.
- Dennis initiates conversations.
- Dennis volunteers for class projects.
- Dennis plays with others.

In summary, she might say to the parents:

- Dennis appears to have adjusted well socially for a second grader.

Another example would be in describing a student's level of knowledge. Rather than saying a student will gain a knowledge of ways to deal with specifics, a teacher might say:

- Michelle will recognize symbols.
- Michelle will be able to cite trends.
- Michelle will be able to cite rules.

SHARE INFORMATION WITH PARENTS.   At the conference, present the parents with as much information about their child as possible. You should have examples of the work to show and explain. You should have test scores available with jargon-free explanations. You may want to provide the parent with a short written supplementary report, so they can take the information home. By providing information to parents, you are demonstrating that you have based your judgments of their child on fact and produced work, not on some subjective possible casual judgment.

INCORPORATE PARENT IDEAS.   Since the IEP conference should involve equal participation from both teacher and parents, allow parents to have a major say in some of the IEP recommendations. It is not only important but also mandated that parents be involved in the educational planning of their children. Listed below are steps you can follow to help incorporate parent ideas into the IEP:

- Have the parents talk about their personal values with regard to education. In this conversation, you need to assess where you feel the parents expect the major focus of the educational treatment to be. Do parents expect their child to be able to function eventually at grade level? Or, do parents expect their child to be pushed to his or her limit in areas of academic skills? How much motivation do the parents have for their child's achievement? These and similar questions should be answered as the parents talk about their personal educational values.

- Once you have a good idea of where the parents expect the educational plan to focus, brainstorm, with them, alternative approaches to remediate the educational deficits. For example, if a parent expects a mentally retarded child to be able to read an adult version of the Bible at the end of the school year, you might offer as an alternative an abridged storybook version. Another parent may insist that resource-room help be available for a child in reading. The teacher may feel that the child might benefit more from a self contained classroom setting. By brainstorming alternatives, you are expanding the parents' view of what might be available to their child.

- The next step is to ask the parents to rank order the objectives they feel are the most important for the year. For some parents, it will be academic growth in a particular area; for other, maturity in a particular area. By placing these objectives in some order, the parent and the teacher can gain a sense of where to focus the school's resources.

HOW TO CONDUCT A SUCCESSFUL BACK-TO-SCHOOL NIGHT

Most schools have evenings that parents can come in to review the course material and meet their child's teacher. Most of these activities occur relatively early in the school year, around the fifth or sixth week of school. For most special-education teachers, these evenings can be lonely ones. It is not rare to find few parents of special-education students coming to these affairs.

There are many reasons for this. It is not the place in this section to discuss these reasons but rather to provide a means whereby you, the teacher, can conduct a back-to-school night that is attended by many, if not most, of the parents.

To begin with, you need to change the format of the evening. Design the activity as a party and with the idea that parents are being invited in a special way to attend. Have the students write personal invitations to their parents. You should also mail home an invitation. Call parents and ask them to bring a cake, some soda, cups, or whatever. If a parent commits him- or herself on the phone to bring something, he or she will most likely show up. Ask each parent to bring his or her child or even all his or her children if they cannot find sitters. You may need to ask each student to bring a parent. In any case, you should have it fixed in your mind that you are going to hustle for the parents to come.

On the day of the event, have the students clean and decorate the room. The students should develop an anticipation of excitement for the coming evening event. Make final phone calls to check on parents who have not yet given an R.S.V.P. Prepare name tags for everyone: students, parents, and yourself.

Figure 3-4 is a sample agenda of activities you may consider conducting during the evening. You need not follow the time schedule exactly. Use this as a guide when you do your specific planning.

"Talk-Behind-Your-Back" Activity

The goal of this activity is to give parents and students an opportunity to listen to each other.

Ask the parents to turn their backs to the group of children. They should be instructed that they are only to listen to what the children have to say. Remind them that it is more important to listen than it is to spend time figuring out who is talking.

Ask the children to respond to these questions:

- What do parents do that you like?
- What do parents do that you dislike?

Allow the students to talk about 15 minutes. If there is a pause in the student discussion, allow it to continue a few minutes. If it seems that there will be no further comments, you might ask some general questions of the students that are based on what they have already said.

The next step is for the students to turn their back on the parents. The students are reminded just to listen and not comment on what is being said. The parents are asked the following questions:

- What does your child do that you like the best?
- What does your child do that you like the least?

After 15 minutes of the parent dialogue, ask the parents to stop.

Ask both groups to face each other. Ask the parents and students what they heard. The comments will tell you what they learned. Have the two groups avoid

SAMPLE AGENDA FOR BACK-TO-SCHOOL NIGHT

Introductions (7:30 p.m.–7:45 p.m.)
Greet each parent at the door to the classroom. Distribute name tags and ask the early arrivals to look around the classroom at some of the projects and students' work, which should be on display. Once everyone has arrived, conduct a formal introduction. Explain what will happen during the evening, and give some estimate of when the affair will be concluded. Ask each student to introduce his or her parent or parents.

Part I (7:45 p.m.–8:00 p.m.)
The first part of the evening should be a demonstration of what you do to help the students learn. Explain the curriculum by describing what students learn in each of the subject areas you teach. Some teachers have produced slide shows to show the various activities of the students. Parents love to see their children in pictures. This slide show can be quite entertaining and can include humor, acting, and staged photos. If the students are mature and old enough, the production of this slide program could make a very rich learning experience for them.

Encourage questions at the end of your presentations. In case the parents do not pose questions, you should be prepared to pose a few yourself and to provide answers. For example, you might say:

"One question to ask is how does this course in social studies differ from what other students in fourth grade learn. Well, the answer is ..."

Part II (8:00 p.m.–8:45 p.m.)
As with any good learning activity, it is a good idea to switch the format and sensory modality you are using at this point. Ask the parents to form a group at one end of the classroom and the students to form a similar group at the other. Introduce the "Talk-Behind-Your-Back" activity by explaining how hard it is to hear and understand the different views of an issue. The activity the group will now conduct allows the parents and the students an opportunity to talk to each other and to share their thoughts and feelings about issues.

Part III (8:45 p.m.–9:00 p.m.)
After this activity, provide time for parents to view the academic work of their child. You could prepare academic folders for the parents and the child to view together. Samples of work, projects, drawings and completed workbook assignments should be included.

Part IV (9:00 p.m.–9:30 p.m.)
Announce that it is refreshment time and that the students will serve the parents. That announcement will bring laughs. The refreshments will help parents stay a bit longer and provide you with time for individual conferences. During this time, you can individualize your remarks and perhaps make appointments for future conferences. It is suggested that you not use this evening for IEP conferences. The tone of the evening should be that of a general introduction and should include a brief overview of the academic and social program.

Figure 3–4

commenting on what individuals said as individuals. Summarize what both groups have said and mention that, perhaps because of this activity, both parents and students have heard things about each other that they have not heard before. Remind them of the goal of this activity and that they could continue the dialogue with each other on their own.

VARIATION FOR YOUNGER STUDENTS.   Younger students will need more structure to move this activity along. You may need to pose questions to the students sitting in a circle. Ask each of them to respond to the question, and then move on to the next question. Sample questions might be:

- What do you think of your parents' rules?
- What bothers you the most about home?
- What do you like the most about home?
- If you could change one thing in your home, what would it be?

HOW TO SOLVE COMMON CLASSROOM PROBLEMS EFFICIENTLY

Aside from the yearly IEP conference, many special-education teachers have great difficulty scheduling additional parent conferences. Many times you need to meet with parents because of particular discipline problems you are experiencing with a student. Quite often, many students in your class share or demonstrate similar disruptive behavior. Time becomes a precious commodity. Rather than call each student's parents in for a conference, why not consider calling all the parents and students in together at the same time.

This multi-family intervention strategy is both economical and extremely efficient in producing student behavior change. By bringing parents together to discuss common concerns and with their child also present, you allow the power of group dynamics to work for you. Both peer group pressure and internal family dynamics pressure are operative here. The power of this strategy is yours because you control the agenda. The next section gives a complete agenda for implementing this strategy and includes a detailed description of each step you should take. Using this formula, you can produce behavior change, quite literally, overnight.

Planning Multi-Family Conferences

Decide on a common problem that a number of your students share. This problem could be behavioral or academic. For our case, let's assume the problem has reached such proportions that the students have begun to become disruptive. Individual counseling and the use of other behavior change strategies have failed to work thus far. While each student may demonstrate his or her disruption differently, classroom patterns of disruption probably exists; that is, students are disrupting your attempts to help them learn.

The agenda described here can work from a range of 20 people to as few as six. The number will vary and depend on how many single-parent families you have present. In any case, a minimum of three families should be used. With fewer, the power of group dynamics will not be operative. If you have problems with the numbers, you may want to consider asking a colleague to invite his or her parents to the meeting, also. After all, this teacher is probably experiencing the same difficulties you are with a few students. Ask the school counselor, social worker, or psychologist to help.

Sending Invitations

Call each parent you would like to invite to this meeting. It is much less anxiety-provoking to a parent when they can discuss the matter with you. Receiving a letter as a form of invitation would be considered too formal. Your call sets the tone. Parents need to know that they will not be blamed for their child's disruptive behavior. They need to be reassured that you need their assistance to help their child. After your call, they should feel that they can offer you something. Below is a sample phone conversation you might want to adapt to meet your needs.

TEACHER: Hello, Mrs. Smith, this is Connie's teacher. As you know, I have been having problems with Connie completing her work in class. She just does not complete all her assignments. I have tried a number of things to motivate and interest her. Nothing works. She completes a few pages of the work while she should be doing five to six. She can do it, but she just refuses. Frankly, Mrs. Smith, I need your help.

MRS. SMITH: Well, of course, I wish to help. There is little I can do. Connie has a mind of her own.

TEACHER: I realize that. However, I have a plan that will work, but I need your cooperation. Could you make an evening meeting with Connie and me? Also, I am inviting a few other parents and their children. All these children have the same problem as Connie. They don't do enough work in class.

MRS. SMITH: Well, I don't know. Can't we just get together tomorrow ourselves? I don't like meetings.

TEACHER: I understand. However, I have tried everything as you know. Meetings are not enough. Besides, the plan I have will produce change by tomorrow. Don't you want to end my calling you and the poor report cards Connie is getting? The other parents, you may know. They all are friendly folks, like yourself. I really need your help.

MRS. SMITH: Okay, I'll try it.

TEACHER: I'll call you in a few days with the time and date. (At this point, you could ask the parent for a few convenient dates. Also, you should consider that a mother, at home, may need to consult with her husband first. Insist that both parents participate.)

Making Introductions

The night of the meeting, have the classroom or meeting facility prepared to greet your guests. You may want to use a conference room rather than a classroom for the general meeting. Many student desks do not seat an adult comfortably. Ideally, a large conference room, with three additional classrooms in the same or general area, would work very well. Distribute name stickers, serve refreshments, and make the introductions. Parents and students need to feel welcomed and put at ease as much as possible.

Prepare and have available some evidence of the students' particular problem. If it is a school-attendance problem, have a school-attendance card for each student. If it is out-of-seat behavior, have a frequency count for each student available. (Refer to a Chapter One section for a description of how to complete a frequency count.) In our case with Connie, the teacher would have samples of work Connie has completed, as well as samples of work not done. The goal here is to be able to confront the student in front of the parent with the facts or data.

The General Meeting

Formally start the meeting by thanking the parents and students for coming. Provide them with a verbal description of the evening's agenda. Make it brief and give an indication of what time the meeting will end. Mention that the goal of the meeting is for each family to leave with an action plan to improve each student's behavior. Reassure the parents that each plan will be unique to their situation. Also thank them for helping you because, without their presence that evening, you would still be having difficulty changing the student.

During this phase of the meeting, you should do most of the talking. The families need to see you as being in charge of this meeting. Remember, they do not necessarily know each other well, and they would most likely become cautious and perhaps fearful if they saw someone else running the show. You are the common factor in this meeting. They trusted you enough to come, so do not disappoint them by allowing the leadership of the meeting to pass out of your hands. Keep the purpose of the meeting in their minds—to help you improve their child's behavior in school.

Setting Up Small Groups

At this point, divide the large group into three separate groups: fathers, mothers and students. You should accompany the student group to serve as group leader. If you have other staff members available, assign one or more to each of the groups. Before the members depart, give the group a task. Tell them they have about 15 or 20 minutes to discuss these questions:

- How do they feel about coming to this meeting?
- What is the problem?
- What has worked at home to improve their child's behavior?

The purpose of these small groups is to allow each member the opportunity to discuss with their peers what positive thing works at home to improve his or her child. This grouping provides support, idea exchange, and an opportunity for everyone to talk. If you are with the students, you need only change the focus a bit.

- What do your parents do at home that helps you behave or follow the rules?

As a group leader, remember to make sure everyone gets a chance to talk. Point out similar ideas, contrast dissimilar ones, and summarize the small group meeting at the end of the time period.

A few dynamics are worth sharing here:

FATHERS' GROUP.   The men may have difficulty talking about the problem. They may make more general statements and avoid feelings. It is usually not common to discuss one's family in front of strangers. As a group leader, acknowledge that these feelings exist.

MOTHERS' GROUP.   Guilt may be the general feeling here. Many mothers feel responsible for the inability of their child to perform well in school. They may question what they could do better to improve the child. As a leader, make sure that the responsibility of the child's behavior does not come to rest with the mothers. Remind them that their child is the one responsible.

STUDENTS' GROUP.   The students will be angry and nervous during this phase. They will try to avoid the task by ignoring the topic, remaining silent, making a joke about it, or promising to improve. As a leader, remember to keep them on-task. Recognize the anger and nervousness if it exists, and mention it to the group.

Establishing a Behavioral Contract

Reassemble the three groups in the general meeting room. Ask each group to summarize their discussion. During this discussion, a numerous feelings will be revealed. Look for them and mention them to the group. In addition, many ideas or successful techniques will be discussed. Parents can get ideas from each other here. If many failure techniques are also mentioned, it is okay. You need to remind the group that you will provide an additional success technique this evening, so it does not matter if all else has failed to change behavior in a family. You have a positive, successful method to offer, in which all parents can participate.

At this point, distribute copies of a behavioral contract (see Form 3-5) to all family units. Ask each family to complete the contract. In a short explanation, also distribute and describe the seven basic steps the family should follow in designing a contract. These basic steps are given in Form 3-6. Essentially, students will be asked to improve in school in order to receive rewards distributed at home. You may want to display examples of contracts previously completed.

At this point, announce to the families that they will begin to negotiate a contract with their child. Each family will complete its own individual contract. Remind the family you are there to assist them design the contract. Have carbon paper or a copy machine available to make copies of this contract. When the contract is completed and everyone has signed off, the family can depart.

Ask each family unit to move to another part of the room or to another room, where they can begin the task of producing a behavior contract. While a contract is the primary goal, a secondary goal is that of opening up family communication. Family members must talk to one another to complete this task. They must reach a compromise, and that demands mutual respect and trust. So while the family will leave with a contract in hand, it also will leave with a unique communication experience.

The contract should be as precise as possible. A planned cause of action should be outlined, with specific consequences mentioned. The contract should be written for a week only. The teacher will report the student's progress, and the parent will dispense the reward, if any. It is more positive to reward progress than to punish failure. For younger children, it is appropriate to provide an extra material incentive. For older children, middle-school-aged and up, there should be no extra rewards for doing what they should anyway. This age group should earn, through positive classroom performance, some of the normal "perks" or special treats parents provide at home. Two sample contracts are given in Figures 3-5 and 3-6 to provide you with some idea of what the final product will look like.

You may need to renegotiate each contract as time goes on. This can be done on the phone. The important thing is that the home and the community are now working together through the behavior change contract to improve a student's behavior.

HOW TO DEAL WITH ANGRY PARENTS

When parents come to school for a conference, the last thing you need is to face an angry parent. This is especially true if that anger is directed at you. Parents have a right to be angry—make no mistake about that. They may even have a right to be mad at you. However, the work to be accomplished at a conference can best be completed if raw emotion is not present. The strategies discussed in this section in no way minimize the right of parents to be angry. What these strategies do offer

AGENDA FOR IEP CONFERENCES

1. *Introduction of persons at meeting.* Parents may want to write down who was present.

2. *Student test results.* The academic, social, psychomotor, medical, and, if appropriate, vocational status of the student will be discussed. The student will be compared in a general way to the developmental progress he or she has made at this point in his or her school career. A summary statement will be made integrating the various evaluation findings and observations.

3. *Discussion of long-range goals* (usually one year). At this point, the teacher will present many goals to describe what objectives the school will strive to achieve with the child during the next year. These goals will be social, behavioral, medical, academic, or vocational. Parents have a right to equal participation in developing these goals. If a parent feels the goals are not approrpriate or realistic, he or she should question the teacher.

4. *Services.* Sometimes services in addition to a classroom teacher will be needed; e.g., counseling, speech and language, or tutorial assistance.

5. *Placement.* Exactly where the child will be placed for the coming school year and for how long each day will be written in the IEP. The teacher should also present placement alternatives and describe why they are not recommended at this time.

6. *Evaluation.* A very clear process should be described to inform the parents how the goals for the coming year will be measured. Specifically, parents should have an idea of whether or not the goals were achieved that is based on the outcome of these measurements. A time table should be given to parents.

Form 3-4

BEHAVORIAL CONTRACT

Name_____ Date_____

Goal for Student

_____

_____

_____

What the Student Will Do

_____

_____

_____

What the Parents Will Do

_____

_____

_____

Witness:_____ Signed:

_____

_____

_____

_____

Form 3-5

SEVEN BASIC STEPS IN NEGOTIATING
A BEHAVIORAL CONTRACT

1. Select one behavior to change. This will be the goal of the student. For example, "The student will come to school on time."

2. Discuss when the problem occurs most. If it is being on time, perhaps one day of the week is worse than other days. Perhaps, it is during a particular class or at a certain time of day.

3. Discuss with the student how this goal can be accomplished. Ask the student what he or she can do to change. You can direct younger children; ask older children for ideas. Refer to the section in the contract titled, "What the Student Will Do."

4. Discuss with the student what the parents will do if the student fulfills his or her part of the previous step. Usually, a reward is given. For example, if a student is on time to school for three days in a row, he or she can have an extra hour to play outside.

5. Write up the behavior contract, indicating what the student will do and what the parent will do. Include, especially, when the teacher will report to the parent whether the behavior was changed.

6. Obtain the necessary signatures to the behavior contract. Stress with the student that his or her word is important, and that this contract should be completed.

7. Establish a review date. Perhaps, after the first week, the teacher can phone the parents to discuss whether revision is needed.

Form 3-6

BEHAVIORAL CONTRACT

Name: __Billy Smith_____   Date: __April 3_____

Goal for Student

__To remain in his seat the entire workbook period after lunch._____

_____

_____

_____

What the Student Will Do

__Billy will not get out of his seat the entire class period when the class__

__is working on their workbooks._____

_____

_____

What the Parents Will Do

__Every night the parents will receive a call from the teacher to find out__

__if Billy did complete his goal. If he completed the goal, he is to be__

__allowed an extra half hour outside to play._____

_____

Witness: __Mrs. Thomas_____   Signed:

                                          _____

                                          _____

                                          _____

                                          _____

                                          _____

Figure 3–5

BEHAVIORAL CONTRACT

Name: _Mary_____   Date: _November 10th_

Goal for Student

_To complete all homework._____

_____

_____

_____

What the Student Will Do

_Each night Mary will show her parents the homework assignments.___

When Mary has completed the assignments, she will show her parents

the completed work.

_____

What the Parents Will Do

_Each night that Mary completes the required assignments, she will be___

allowed to stay at her friend Sue's house for one half hour on Saturday.

_____

_____

Witness: _Mrs. Thomas_____   Signed:

_____

_____

_____

_____

_____

Figure 3–6

you, however, are procedures to cope with the anger, and methods to redirect the conference back to ways that help the student. Five different methods are described here.

It is suggested that you practice each method and then decide which one is most appropriate to your style and personality. There may be times during a parent conference that you could employ a number of these methods. If you do so, make sure that you use the methods not as a desperate search for one that works but rather as a means of continually de-escalating the anger. Examples from actual parent conferences will be used here to illustrate how to use each method and how to use the methods in concert.

Ignore It

You hear the parent being angry and feel the anger being projected at you, but you actually ignore it and do not give any indication that you received it. What happens here is that the parent is not hurt by his or her anger directed at you, and you are not forced to respond to a negative situation. The anger is dissipated and causes no harm. Here is an example:

> PARENT: Why are you always picking on my son? Do you not like my son? That's it. You really don't like him, do you? Well, I don't like you either.
>
> TEACHER: As I was saying, we really need to get Ricky into school more often. He needs to learn. He is a bright boy.

Here the teacher heard and felt the parent's anger but decided to ignore it and move on with her agenda. The teacher had to harden herself to deal with this direct attack, but she made a decision that the goal of the conference was Ricky's school attendance and not the mother's feelings toward her or the school. Most likely, in this case, the mother is projecting her own feelings of frustration for Ricky onto the teacher. But that is a concern for another procedure discussed later; it's called, "Redirect It."

Agree with It

If you agree with the parent's anger, then you will find that you have established a process that justifies this anger and thereby reduces its strength. This method does not ask you to agree with the reasons for the anger, only with the fact that the parent is mad. There is a subtle difference here. You do not want to get into a discussion of agreeing or disagreeing with the parent about why he or she is angry. What you want to do is to agree to the fact that the parent is expressing anger. If you agree with the feeling, you are justifying and validating the anger for the parent. The result will be a reduction in the intensity of the anger, and a reduction in the parent's guilt for surfacing the anger.

> PARENT: The teachers in the building are lousy. You top the list. There are times I want to shake you from head to toe.
>
> TEACHER: There are a lot of people here, parents and students, who would like to shake me. I regret that I make you feel so angry.

What the teacher has accomplished using this process is to agree with the fact of the anger without having to engage in it. The teacher, essentially, has told the parent it is okay to be angry at her.

Another variation of this same procedure is to say outright that you agree with the parent. This is a more overt form of agreement, and its result is much more dramatic. For example, in responding to the parent above, the teacher could have said,

> "Yes, I agree with you. There are times I am not the best. I have days I slip a bit."

The effect here is to cloud the aggression of the parent. What can the parent say to this remark? Certainly, the parent would be hard pressed to continue the attack. There is no longer any disagreement.

Redirect It

Once the parent has expressed the anger, the teacher can take charge of it and direct it onto something else or someone else. This redirection reduces the immediate threat to the teacher and quite literally dumps the anger somewhere else. For example:

> PARENT: My son would have no problems in this school if only the others would stop bothering him. They always pick on him. He allows it. Why do you allow this to go on? You are the teacher. Do something.
>
> TEACHER: I would be mad too if he were my son. The way this class is organized, I have so many different types of children that it is hard to keep them all cooperating at all times.

The teacher now has directed the anger onto the schedule. The parent was angry at the teacher for failing to manage the class, while the teacher has now placed the anger onto something more structural.

This redirection of anger can also be used to place anger onto another. This is a bit tricky, because it involves pulling a third party into the scene. However, this procedure could be used if, indeed, a third party is responsible for this anger or situation. Using our previous example, the teacher could say,

"Perhaps you are angry at your son a bit for allowing others to pick on him. Perhaps you feel he needs to take charge more often here."

Here the teacher is redirecting the mother's anger toward her son. The teacher made an educated guess because of a remark the parent made initially; the parent said, "He allows it."

Once you have redirected the anger, you will know whether you have succeeded if the parent then picks up on this and proceeds to discuss the new direction. You are now free of the personal intensity of the attack and can focus on helping the parent resolve the anger.

Counterattack

Sometimes you may feel that the parent's attack is so misguided and inappropriate that you feel you need to respond. The trick here is not to attack the parent verbally. That would only escalate the situation. Your goal in a counterattack is to neutralize the anger by confronting it head on. You do this by commenting on the verbal statements, examples, or words used by the parent. For example:

> PARENT: I have had it. All we do is talk. Talk. Talk. I have been in this school three years now, and my son still is having problems. Do your job! Teach him to read, to get a job, to be a man!
>
> TEACHER: Now let's stop right here. I am working hard. I am using all the skills I know. I know a lot about teaching. There are some things I can do with your son. I can help him to read. I cannot help him get a job. I cannot help him be a man.

The teacher confronts the parent by directing her to stop the attack. He then musters up his self-confidence to tell the parent what he can and cannot do. He responds to her specific demands, one by one. This method demands that the teacher by self-confident, organized, and focused on the discussion. By sheer power of the response, the teacher can disarm the parent with this type of counterattack.

Make It Absurd

This method, based on Carl Whitaker's "Psychology of the Absurd: With Specific Emphasis on Psychotherapy of Aggression" (*Family Process, 14,* March 1975), is quite different from the rest, because it is based on escalating rather than reducing the parent's anger. This may sound strange and dangerous, but if you keep a few rules in mind, you will find yourself in total control.

The first thing to remember is that you do not want to resolve the conflicting anger by searching for a peaceful solution, but rather seek to force the parent to extend the anger to its extreme dimension. The seven steps are as follows:

1. The parent presents anger.
2. The teacher accepts the anger and adds to it.
3. The parent responds to the addition.
4. The teacher responds to the parent's remark by adding further to the anger.
5. The parent tries to evade the escalation of the anger.
6. The teacher adds again.
7. There is a break in the parent's thought pattern, and the anger and all its additions collapse.

An example of the use of these seven steps follows:

Step 1—Parent: Teachers, including you, in this building cannot teach.

Step 2—Teacher: You could be right. There are few "master" teachers in this world.

Step 3—Parent: You said it. There are none here. I am sure.

Step 4—Teacher: There may be none here. None anywhere in this city. Finding "masters" is hard. You may have to move to another city to find what you want.

Step 5—Parent: I do not want to move.

Step 6—Teacher: As a matter of fact, the more I think about it, the more I feel you are right. You should begin an immediate search for the best teachers. Be prepared to move though. As you said, there are none to be found here.

Step 7—Parent: Now wait a minute. You are crazy. I am not moving. Let's talk about my son doing better here in this school.

Once the absurdity reaches a point where the parent's thought pattern is broken, there are a number of ways that parents cope. In our example, the absurdity becomes evident, for it brings the parent back to task. The parent sees through it and takes the opportunity to bring the conference back to its original focus—her son. Another common outcome is for the parent to recognize the absurdity, become increasingly angry at you, and leave the conference. At first, this may seem like a disaster for a conference. However, you made your point and told the parent you would not tolerate anger being directed at you. The next conference with this parent will mostly likely be void of any anger. A third coping response results when the absurdity does not become evident. Parents have no idea what you are doing, but take your absurdity to heart.

Once these parents try to implement your unrealistic recommendation, however, they will find themselves in a situation where they will need to come back for help. In our example, the parent would have begun researching which local cities had better teachers. She would have soon given up this impossible task and returned to the immediate task of helping her son in his local school.

Illustrated here is an example of a teacher using a number of strategies to deal with a parent's anger. Read how the teacher takes a display of nasty anger and, through a verbal dialogue, de-escalates it so that the parent is ready and capable of talking about problems his child is having in school.

PARENT:	[To teacher] We are going to talk. I will talk. You will listen.	
TEACHER:	Sit down, Mr. Smith. I am glad you came in to talk about your son. I know this is an inconvenient time for you.	[Ignore it.]
PARENT:	It sure is. I am going to get to the point. Why suspend him for something he did not do?	
TEACHER:	I did not suspend him. I cannot suspend.	[Redirect it.]
PARENT:	Well, who did? I want to settle this.	
TEACHER:	The principal suspends.	[Redirect it.]
PARENT:	Get him in here.	
TEACHER:	I will. Before I do so, you need to have some facts. One, your son had a four-inch knife on him. Two, he displayed it publicly. Three, the rules say a student will be suspended for carrying a knife.	[Counterattack]
PARENT:	What's a four-inch knife going to do? He won't kill anyone.	
TEACHER:	Well, would you say a five-inch knife could kill someone?	[Begins making it absurd, Step 2]
PARENT:	Why, sure. But a knife doesn't mean you have to suspend.	[Step 3]
TEACHER:	I know. But let's take away the rule about knives in school. Any student can bring in a knife. In fact, we'll put up notices saying that this rule needs to be dropped. We'll encourage everyone to bring a knife to protect themselves from everyone else.	[Step 4]
PARENT:	Wait a minute.	[Step 5]

TEACHER: Could you help us with the   [Step 6]
publicity on this? You believe
strongly that a kid should not be
suspended and that everyone
should have a knife in school.

PARENT: Okay, okay. I realize what you   [Step 7]
are doing. This is nuts. We are
talking about knives in school.

TEACHER: Can we talk about your son and
the homework he'll need to do
when he is suspended?

HOW TO REDUCE STUDENT TELEVISION VIEWING

Every teacher knows that after-school study time and reading time are in direct competition with after-school television viewing time. Children would prefer to turn on a TV set than open up a book. There has been much discussion about what influence TV has on the minds of our young children. Many parents find controlling the viewing habits of their children a very difficult task. Latchkey and older children often get home before their parents, and thus they have even more unlimited access to TV viewing. Teachers are often asked for assistance from parents in reducing TV viewing time for their children. The technique described here will provide a teacher with a very specific way in which to reduce TV viewing habits. This technique can easily be taught to parents.

One of the chief problems in controlling TV viewing is the lack of control on the presence of the set. Unlike trying to control other habits where the "temptation" can even be kept from the house, almost no parent will accept the idea of eliminating the TV set. So the task is not to control the absence or presence of the set, but to control the *time* used for viewing.

To do this, children can be given tokens each week to "buy" TV viewing time. These tokens can be used to "purchase" any TV show the child wants. Depending on how many hours of TV a child watches each week, the parent can adjust the amount of tokens up or down. Let's assume that a child watches an average of 24 hours of TV a week—the national average, incidentally. If a parent wished to cut this amount in half, he or she would offer a certain number of tokens that, if all used, would only "buy" a total of 10 hours per week of TV viewing.

Since most television shows are one half hour in length, it is best to have a particular token that is worth one half hour of TV viewing. The tokens themselves could be poker chips, play money coins, or even checker pieces. At the start of the week, give the child all twenty tokens. Tell the child that these can be used to purchase time to watch TV. Ask the child to plan ahead and to decide which shows are more important than others. Make sure to give the token its worth; e.g., one token equals one half hour or one hour. Every time the child wants to watch TV, he or she must give a parent one token. The parent must supervise the TV to make sure that the TV set is turned off at the end of the allocated time.

This system may seem like punishment to the child. The parent, however, can add a reward system. For example, if the child completes the token buying system successfully at the end of the week, then he or she can be rewarded. This reward could range from a trip to the toy store, ice-cream store, movie house, or it could be whatever treat a child might desire.

From experience, there are a few items to look for in advising parents about this technique.

1. Both parents must agree to the procedure and agree not to give extra tokens during the week.

2. If the child comes into a room where the set is on, he or she must purchase time to stay.

3. All children in the house need to be on this system for it to seem fair and to work.

4. Have the parents keep records of what shows were watched, when, and for how long. This information could be shown to the child as feedback about what he or she likes on TV.

5. If a child has access to a TV when parents are not at home (latchkey or older children), this procedure will not work. A TV equipped with a lock could be used to prevent after-school use. If this is not possible, use the token procedure only for times when the parents are at home. In this case, drastically reduce the number of tokens given.

There are definite consequences of this procedure that should be noted. First, since the child now has more free time because of his or her reduction in TV viewing, it is possible for study or reading time to increase. Parents should encourage their children to pursue educational activities during this extra time. Keeping a record of activities is also helpful for the parent. (Refer to Form 3-7, which is described below.) The second consequence of this procedure is that, over a period of time, a child may actually grow used to less TV viewing time. At some later date, the token system can be removed; most likely the child will not return to the previous amount of TV viewing time.

Form 3-6 is a weekly progress chart a parent can use to measure the effectiveness of the procedure to reduce a child's television viewing time. Make copies of the form, and distribute them to the parents.

The next logical step is to match school resources with the ranked objectives concluded in the previous step. Parents at this point need to know the alternatives to any recommendations a teacher is making. For example, if it has been determined that the child's behavior needs the major emphasis for the next school year and that place-

WEEKLY PROGRESS CHART OF CHILD'S TV VIEWING

Week of _____   Student's Name _____

	Number of Tokens Used	TV Shows Watched	Activities When Not Watching TV
Monday			
Tuesday			
Wednesday			
Thursday			
Friday			

Form 3-7

ment in a local-building, special-education class will meet this need, parents should also be made aware of other alternative classes or special-education programs outside the local building, or even school district, that could possibly meet these needs. However, a teacher also needs to explain why he or she feels that the first recommendation is the best for the child. In our example here, the best reason to accept a local school-building placement is that it offers the least restrictive environment.

- The final step is to determine when you and the parents feel a particular goal will be achieved. For most educational programs, the end of the school year would be an appropriate period. This final step, however, can provide the teacher with some flexibility if he or she feels that a particular parent recommendation to this point is not appropriate for the child. Any objective can be tried for a short period of trial to determine its appropriateness. If a parent really insists that their learning-disabled child, for example, can handle an honors math class in seventh grade, perhaps this objective should be given a trial period. A time limit of first report card for this course could be established.

Summing Up

To summarize this section on how to improve IEP conferences, the teacher needs to respect the needs and rights of parents to become full partners in the educational planning of their child. This respect for parent choices ranges from the parent who just wants to review an IEP written beforehand by the teacher to the parent who wants to have a major say in what goes into an IEP. This respect for choices should also include a parent who never comes to a single conference. In order to assist parents in becoming full partners, Form 3-4 is a sample agenda for IEP conferences that a teacher could distribute to parents before the conference. After looking at this sample, a teacher may wish to alter it to meet his or her particular school-district situation.

WHERE TO SEEK FURTHER HELP

Very often, parents will ask you for sources from which they can receive further information about or even help with their particular child's handicapped condition. A partial listing of agencies or groups that can provide such assistance follows:

Association for Children with Learning Disabilities
4156 Library Road
Pittsburgh, PA 15234

Association for Educational Therapists
P.O. Box 946
Woodland Hills, CA 91365

Big Brothers/Big Sisters of America
117 South 17th Street, Suite 1200
Philadelphia, PA 19103

Children's Defense Fund
122 C Street, N.W.
Washington, D.C. 20001

Council for Exceptional Children
1920 Association Drive
Reston, VA 22091

Foundation for Children with Learning Disabilities
99 Park Avenue
New York, NY 10016

National Center for Missing and Exploited Children
1835 K Street, N.W., Suite 700
Washington, D.C. 20006

National Clearinghouse on Child Abuse and Neglect
P.O. Box 1192
Washington, D.C. 20013

National Network of Runaway and Youth Services
905 Sixth Street, S.W., Suite 612
Washington, D.C. 20024

Orten Dyslexia Society
724 York Road
Baltimore, Maryland 21204

CHAPTER 3 REFERENCES

Albert, Linda. *Coping With Kids and School: A Guide for Parents.* New York: E. P. Dutton, 1984.

Erickson, Gerald, and Terrence Hogan (eds.). *Family Therapy.* Monterey, CA: Brooks/Cole Publishing, 1981.

Foundation for Children with Learning Disabilities (FCLD). *Resource Guide: A State-by-State Directory of Special Programs, Schools, and Services.* New York: New York University Press, 1985.

Fulmaer, Richard H., Susan Cohen, and Gail Monaco. "Using Psychological Assessment in Structural Family Therapy." *Journal of Learning Disabilities, 18,* 1985, 145-149.

Goldstein, Susan, Bonnie Strickland, Ann Turnbull, and Lynn Curry. "An Observational Analysis of an IEP Conference." *Exceptional Children, 46,* 1980, 278-286.

Gurman, Alan S., and David P. Kniskern (eds.). "Skill Training Programs for Couples and Families" in *Handbook of Family Therapy.* New York: Brunner/Mazel, 1981.

Lightfoot, Sara Lawrence. *Worlds Apart, Relationships between Families and Schools.* New York: Basic Books, 1978.

Painting, Donald. *Helping Children with Specific Learning Disabilities; A Practical Guide for Parents and Teachers.* Englewood Cliffs, NJ: Prentice Hall, 1983.

Patterson, G. R. *Living with Children: New Methods for Parents and Teachers.* Champaign, IL: Research Press, 1979.

Schaefer, Charles, James M. Briesmeister, and Maureen E. Fitton. *Family Therapy Techniques for Problem Behaviors of Children and Teenagers.* San Francisco: Jossey-Bass, 1984.

Schleifer, Maxwell J., and Stanley D. Klein (eds.). *The Disabled Child and the Family.* Boston: Exceptional Parent Press, 1985.

chapter 4

ACTIVITIES TO IMPROVE HOW STUDENTS FEEL ABOUT THEMSELVES

This chapter is unique in that it can be viewed as an entire course curriculum. The chapter is organized in a ten-month sequence starting with September and ending with June. Each month has at least four class activities described in some detail.

The focus of this chapter is to provide the teacher with activities that, over the course of the year, will generate changes in students, particularly changes in how they feel about themselves. To accomplish this task, the activities in this chapter are designed to develop student skills in a number of areas. Research has shown that a positive self-concept is built on skills, such as the ability to trust others, to understand one's feelings, to be aware of one's values, to know how to handle stress, to be able to communicate and to listen, to be able to understand one's role with others, and, last, to be able to accomplish a task successfully. The reader will find that each of these skills is developed through the activities described in this chapter. Each month, in fact, is devoted to a particular skill area. The activities in this chapter are sequenced to build upon each other; activities performed in September are at the initial stages of developing a positive feeling, while those activities performed in May and June are the final product of nine months of accumulated skill development. A month-by-month description of the different themes is listed below:

- September: Development of basic interpersonal relationship skills and trust

- October: Improvement of self-concept
- November: Advanced development of interpersonal skills
- December: Awareness of values as related to self-concept
- January: Development of social life skills
- February: Development of listening and communication skills
- March: Coordination of interpersonal support and help
- April: Awareness of group pressure
- May: Application of developed skills
- June: Analysis and synthesis of skill development

In terms of a course curriculum most of these activities have been designed to be completed in about 45 minutes. There are some activities that will take longer for students to complete. A few may take a whole week. In general, however, you can plan on using the material in this course in 45-minute blocks. If the course is offered once a week for the entire year, you may wish to give students credit for the work accomplished.

You will need to adapt some of the material depending on the age and mental ability of the students. Most of the material can easily be used from the third-grade level with dull-normal to above-average ability-level students. Some suggestions are made in the different activities to help you adapt some of the material. After each activity has been done, write notes about what happened during the activity, and record any changes that might be incorporated into the activity the next time you use it.

ACTIVITIES FOR SEPTEMBER

The focus for the first month of school is to help students develop strong positive interpersonal relationships with each other. By this, we mean the students in the class should demonstrate mutual cooperation, dependency, and bonding. The specific objectives of this month's activities are directed at teaching students how to initiate and conduct discussions with other classmates, how to develop self-discipline, and how to take risks in forming new relations with others.

Activity 1: Talk Behind Your Back

GOAL: To teach students how to open a discussion with another person, how to exchange information, how to listen, and how to report information.

PROCEDURE: Ask the students to look around the classroom and select a student that they do not know well. Tell the students that they will be interviewing another student in a few minutes and to decide now if the person that they picked is one that they would like to interview. Talk to the class about the need to find information about someone that they do not know well. Speak of the risk involved and about how it may feel uncomfortable at first to talk to this person. Encourage and praise students who pair up with a classmate that they do not know that well. If the class resists pairing, then inform the students that you will make the pairs if they do not. For younger children, you may need to make the pairs.

Ask the pairs of students to find a place in the room where they can talk without interfering with others. Once this is settled, ask one student in each pair to start the interview. Tell the students that they each have three minutes to conduct an interview. After this time, the students switch, and the other student conducts an interview for three minutes. Tell the students that they will be reporting to the class what they heard their partner say. As the teacher, you should also be included in the interview process. You are the model.

Typical questions that students could use for the interview are the following: "What is your favorite movie, video, song, group, record album, sports team, course, hobby?" Questions about the family are good beginnings. Here are some good examples: "How many brothers and sisters do you have? What room is your favorite in the house? What room do you dislike? What is the best place to go to feel relaxed? Who is your best friend? Where do you go on vacation?"

During the interviews, you will need to keep time. Announce when the time is up and when it is time to switch partners. At the end of the interviews, ask the students to form a large circle. Tell the class that, at this time, each student will tell the others what he or she has learned about their partner. The trick in making this report-out, however, is that the speaker will have to stand behind the student interviewed and put his or her hands on the partner's shoulders. The person will introduce the partner and pretend to become that person. He or she will have to use the word "I" rather than, "He said," or, "She likes." For example, Betty interviewed Riette and found out that she likes the color green. Betty then stands behind Riette, puts her hands on Riette's shoulders, and says, "I think my favorite color is green."

This type of report-out can be threatening to students, so encourage and praise students to do it. If the case calls for it, then you go first to break the ice. Also tell students that the sooner they make their report-out, the sooner they will get it over with. Remind them that waiting only makes the tension worse. Once a few do it, the others will follow. Make sure that each pair of students interview back-to-back before you move on to the next pair.

The follow-up to this activity—once everyone goes—is to ask students how they felt. Recognize feelings of embarrassment and fear as well as those of pride and excitement. Meaningful discussions can take place about what went on inside each student's head as they were being talked about. Comments about what students have in common and how they differ should be made. Finally, since listening is such an important part of this activity, you should discuss how hard or easy it was for students to remember things that were said during the interview.

Activity 2: Class Picnic

GOAL: To teach students how to further develop interpersonal trust and informal relations; to demonstrate the interdependency of the class members; and to demonstrate how a task can be planned, organized, and executed.

PROCEDURE: At first, you may wonder whether it is worth taking a whole day to go on a picnic and what a picnic has to do with learning. The best way to answer this question is to look upon the whole experience as a kinesthetic learning experience. The students will be learning by doing.

The first step is to show students how to plan for a task. Post a list of committees that will be needed. Setup, firemaking, cooking, cleaning, and pickup are a few suggested ones. As students sign up for these committees, make sure that all the girls do not get on the same committees, and all the boys on the others. If possible and to reduce costs, ask each student to bring something to the picnic. The food items should be posted on a sign-up basis so that there is no duplication and no essential items missing. You might even negotiate with the school cafeteria for some of food items or for box lunches.

Depending on the age of your children, you will need to structure the day. Provide board games and sports equipment so that groups of students can play together. Sometime during the day, organize an activity in which all can partici-pate—softball, football, sack race, volleyball, etc.

There is no need to have the students summarize their feelings about this day. Their shared participation in the event is sufficient. The trust and respect de-veloped during the day will be carried back to the classroom.

Activity 3: Class Mural

GOAL: To help students gain an understanding of themselves; to help students express this understanding to others; to help students gain an under-standing of how everyone in the class can share common characteristics.

PROCEDURE: This activity involves the students in painting a wall mural. Probably one formal class session will be needed to organize and explain the purpose of the activity. After this introduction, however, the project can be an excellent filler activity for a student who has finished all his or her work and has some free time. It also has potential to serve as a student reinforcer or motivator; students may desire to complete their desk work so that they can continue with the painting project.

Select a wall in your class that is clear of any major objects. A large flat-wall expanse is excellent. Have each student stand in front of a high-power lightbulb or slide projector that can be used to project the student's silhouette onto the wall. Have another student trace the projected silhouette onto the wall. Have students use step ladders so that the different silhouettes can be placed over the entire wall surface. Some of the silhouettes can be drawn close together; some can be related in pictorial scenes. For example, a student may want to show his face a few inches from another student's face, or to show his arm on another's head, or to include an object of common interest together with the silhouettes.

Once the silhouettes begin to be traced, hold a class discussion on how to paint them in. The school art teacher could be a valuable help with ideas and designs. Encourage the students to fill in their murals in a manner that best expresses themselves. Pictures of hobbies, special interests, animals, or even horoscopes may be placed within each silhouette. Use latex water-soluble paint, for otherwise the school principal will have great problems appreciating the meaning of your project. Depending on the age of your children, you may need to touch up a project here and there. Keep the project on display for the entire school year. If new students come into the class, ask them to place their mural up on the wall.

An alternative to not using a whole wall would be for the students to place their silhouettes on 1/8 inch masonite board. The completed boards could be hung from the wall or ceiling. At the end of the school year, the students could take them home.

Activity 4: Killer Game

GOAL: To help students learn how to maintain eye contact; to develop self-discipline; to take risks.

PROCEDURE: The name of this game may strike you as a bit too aggressive. Many students like the name of this game however, for its name adds to the game's excitement and attractiveness. If you are uncomfortable with the name however, then simply change it to meet your needs.

Ask the students to sit in a circle around a table. One student, who is the dealer, gives everyone one card face-down from a regular card deck. The ace of spades is the killer card and must be included in at least one of the cards dealt. Everyone in the game must sit with their hands in front of them. No one is allowed to talk. The students are asked to look and hold the card dealt to them so that no one can see the card they have. The student with the ace of spades is the killer.

The object of the game for the killer is to "knock off" as many other people as possible by simply winking at them with both eyes. This wink should be done as quickly and secretly as possible, so that others at the table do not see it. Individuals who receive a wink from another student are instructed to turn over their card and are officially out of the game. They must remain seated and cannot acknowledge who the killer is. The killer receives points for each person he or she "knocks off."

The object of the game for students who do not have the ace of spades is to determine who the killer is before the killer winks at them. If a student thinks he or she knows who the killer is then the student must ask another player at the table for backup. If another student backs the player, then the player tells the group who he or she thinks the killer is. If the student and the backup are right, they both are credited with killing the killer, and they receive points. If, however, they are wrong, they both lose and must turn over their cards.

This game can be played out over a week or series of weeks, with points recorded for each student. The student at the end of the month with the most points receives a prize.

Adaptation for Activity 4: Indian Chief

Place all the students in a large circle where everyone can see each other eye to eye.

A student is asked to volunteer to be "It." This person then leaves the room. When the student leaves, the teacher selects another student to be the leader, or the Indian chief. This student is instructed to lead the group using nonverbal hand and body motions. The chief can continue to change motions as many times as he or she wants. The student outside the room is called back in. This person's task is to stand in the circle and try to figure out and guess who the leader or the chief is. He or she has three guesses to pick the leader.

ACTIVITIES FOR OCTOBER

While last month's activities dealt with interpersonal relations, the activities for this month move more toward the individual student. The student is asked to look more closely at him- or herself. Research indicates that students perform better academically when they have a positive self-concept. For this reason, the activities of this month are focused at helping students judge themselves in relation to others in the class. These activities help them learn how to feel good about who they are, how to view themselves as sharing in the human condition, and how to determine their own personal strengths and weaknesses.

Activity 1: Self-Collage

GOAL: To help students further define who they are to themselves, and to express this knowledge to others.

PROCEDURE: This project may take several class periods. Tell the students that they are about to make a collage of themselves. To do this, they will be cutting pictures and words out of magazines and newspapers. Ask them to look for pictures and words that they feel best describe who they are, what they are thinking, and what they are feeling. The first class devoted to this activity should be for the students to page through newspapers and magazines. Provide pieces of large oaktag paper or poster paper on which the students may glue the items found.

This activity is usually great fun for students. You may need to help younger children with this project. For older children, you may find yourself involved in discussions helping students to focus on themselves, so they can decide what picture best describes them. Classmates may wish to help in the decisions. In either case, the activity will generate a process of self-discovery that is very rewarding to students.

Once everyone has completed their collages, ask each student to stand in front of the class and describe it. The student should talk about each item on the collage poster. Encourage the other students to ask questions about the items.

As a summary activity, you may want to show students in what way some of the collages are similar, and how they differ. By keeping the focus on the collages, you are talking to the entire class about how students view themselves, but you don't embarrass anybody. This is a very powerful enriching activity that a class of students can go through. Much information is expressed and shared among classmates.

Activity 2: Time-Line

GOAL: To teach students that despite dissimilar experiences, they all share the same basic human realities of life (needs, loves, challenges, beliefs, and joys).

PROCEDURE: The purpose of this activity is to prepare a time chart that illustrates major events in a student's life. Depending on the age of the child, the range of the time-line will be determined. Many students cannot remember many major events that happened in their lives. Part of their disability is in the process of long-term memory. You will have to judge how far back the time-line should start.

Below is an illustration of a time-line for a one-month period for a 10- year-old child:

- April 7: My family bought a new video recorder.
- April 11: I was home from school, because I was sick.
- April 13: I returned to school, and everyone was happy.
- April 20: I got an "A" in social studies.
- April 22: I watched "Annie" on TV. Great movie!
- April 23: I asked my mother if I could dance in school.
- April 28: I had a fight in school and was sent home.

Another student may keep a diary for a while for a student who has difficulty remembering, so that the events in that student's life can be recorded on a time-line. Older students may possibly choose a time-line that spans a number of years.

When all students have completed their time-lines, then have each student stand in front of the class to discuss his or her chart. Ask other students in the class if they can relate to the experiences, or whether they have had similar or dissimilar ones. Ask the students if there was one event in their life that had a major impact. What was it? How did it affect them?

After a period of common discussion, you could then list on the board the words, "Needs, Loves, Challenges, Beliefs, and Joys." Ask the students to put some of the experiences each has had under the word they feel best describes the event. For example, the girl in our illustration might put getting a family video recorder as one of the joys in her monthly time-line. Once you have a good sampling of events under each word, then point out to students that many of the events in their lives can be classified as a common human experience. You can point out that even if the events are different, the experience of life is basically the same. Show the students how we all have needs, loves, challenges, beliefs and joys.

Activity 3: Who Are You?

GOAL: To help students define and identify strengths and weaknesses; to determine which strengths are best, and which weaknesses need to be changed.

PROCEDURE: Tell the students that you are going to ask them ten questions for which they will need a large piece of paper. Ask them to number from one to ten on the page. Then say to the students, "Who are you?" Tell the students that they should write one word, a noun or an adjective, to answer this question. Then repeat the question nine more times. The students should have ten answers on their papers by now.

Ask the students to review their answers to the question, "Who am I?", and to relist them with the most likable adjective or noun placed first on the list, and the least likable placed last.

Now draw a large outline of a person on the board. Tell the class that you are going to fill this person with the best qualities that the students have on their papers. Ask each class member to write his or her best quality—it should be the first item on the reordered list—on a small piece of paper and to pass this information forward to you. Ask an aide or another student to write the words handed up inside the outline of the person drawn on the board. Typical words that might be written within the person's outline are "happy, lover, good, kind, and smart."

Hold a discussion about this new person created from the entire class. Ask the students why they picked the word that they did. Ask the students if one quality is more important than another quality, and why. This discussion will add richness to the understanding of who a person is.

Now draw another diagram of a person. Announce to the class that just as the first character contains all the best qualities of students, this second character will contain all the qualities least-liked. Again ask the students to write on a piece of paper the quality that they have written that is their least likable quality—it should be Number 10 on their reordered list. Have the students pass the word up to the front of the room; as before, record the words inside the diagram. Typical words may be "Dumb, Ugly, Selfish, and Alone." Hold a discussion about these words as you did with the best qualities.

Now point out to the students that there are two people on the board. One contains all that we like about ourselves, and the other contains all that we do not like. Ask the students to surrender one more of their qualities that they have listed on their paper—they should have 8 left. This quality, tell them, should go to the person on the board whom they feel needs it the most. Most of the time, students will surrender a good quality to the diagram that contains all that is disliked, so this person will now have a mixture of those qualities that are liked and disliked.

You can now hold a very interesting discussion with the students about these two diagrams. Ask the students which diagram best illustrates the true student in the class or in the school. Ask the students what it is like being one of these people. Ask them if they think that someone like the first person exists in the school building. Focus questions around the four basic human realities that were discussed in Activity 2 (needs, challenges, loves, beliefs, joys).

The final activity that is part of this discussion is for the students to each pick one quality from those written on the board, and to add it to their list in front of them. You may want to hold a discussion about why an individual picked such and such a quality.

This activity may take more than a class period. It certainly is a good idea to continue it another day if the students really respond to its meaning. Also, later in the school year, you may want to return to it to see if a student has chosen another quality that he or she would like to share with the class.

Activity 4: Fantasy Island

GOAL: To teach students how to set goals; how to determine what additional strengths they would like to have; and how to feel relaxed.

PROCEDURE: Ask each student to close his or her eyes and to relax in the seat. The following narrative could be read to the students, or you could make up your own version to meet the needs of the students.

> "Close your eyes... relax... everything is to be placed out of your mind... school... friends... Nothing at all is to be any part of your thoughts. It is a beautiful day...The sun is out...You are happy to be in a place where there is nothing but mountains, the greenest of grass you have ever seen, the most beautiful flowers you can ever imagine...And you are there all alone. You have just arrived at a fantasy island where everyone's wish comes true. It is such a good feeling. As you walk down the road, you come to a small store. You wonder what is inside. As you come closer, you notice that it is a weird looking place. You decide to enter, and you discover that the store is a magic shop. In this store, you can have three wishes for free. Look around... You can wish for the future, a new personality, friends, anything you wish. You look around... What is it that you want to become as a person? What do you want to change about yourself? You look at all the samples, all the possibilities that you can become as a person. You decide what you want.

When you go up to the man behind the counter, he says you can wish for three things, but you must give three things away. What could these be? He explains that, to add three new things to your personality, you need to give three things away about yourself that you do not like. If you do not have three things about yourself that you do not like, then you have to share three beautiful things about yourself with others, so that they can benefit by your strengths.

You now decide what these things will be. ... You collect your three new wishes and leave the store.

As you walk back down the road, you feel like a new person. The day seems brighter, and, for some reason, it looks and feels better than before. You are walking back to the plane that will take you away from fantasy island. You close your eyes, and you are back at your school ... It is time to wake up."

Follow the narrative with a group discussion.

- Ask the student how they felt.
- Ask the students what their three wishes were.
- Ask the students what they gave up to receive these wishes.
- Mention to students that, although this was a fantasy island trip, it could be real if they would like to work on making it real. You might want to describe how one student's wish could be made real as an example to others in the class.
- Develop the theme "If you can dream it, you can do it." (This is the motto of the General Electric Corporation.)

ACTIVITIES FOR NOVEMBER

This month's activities are designed to have the student return to the focus of the interpersonal relationships in the class. In contrast to the September activities, in which interpersonal relations were first emphasized, this month's activities require a student to increase his or her involvement with others in the classroom. Specific objectives are directed at helping students understand how they function in a group, how they make decisions with others, how words can hurt and help, and how to help another.

Activity 1: Man-Tiger-Gun

GOAL: To demonstrate the need for cooperation and group consensus when the class has to make a decision.

PROCEDURE: Separate the class into two teams, with equal numbers on each side. Also choose one observer for each team. Ask the two teams to move to opposite corners of the room. The object of this activity is for the team to decide if it wants to represent a man, a tiger, or a gun. To represent each of these roles, instruct each member of the team to do the following:

- Man: Cross arms across your chest.
- Tiger: Place arms over your head, curl your hands as claws, and growl.
- Gun: Extend arms out from shoulder height, as if you were shooting a gun.

Ask each team to decide upon which role it would like to represent. Inform the students that, when you give the signal, both teams are to move to the center of the room, and that at your next signal, every team member will have to demonstrate the agreed-upon position.

Certain positions "win" over certain other positions:

- Man wins over gun
- Gun wins over tiger
- Tiger wins over man

Depending on the age of your students, you may need to explain why each of these roles wins over a particular other role.

Inform your students that the objective of the activity is to gain points for each win your team makes over the opposing team. If both teams assume the same role, then the round is a tie. If any team member assumes a role different from the other on the team, then the team loses the round, even if the team's role would have won.

Ask if there are questions. Ask each team to decide in secret what role it will assume: man, tiger, or gun. Give the signal to advance, and the signal to assume a role. Award points to the winning team. Then ask the teams to withdraw and think of another strategy to win the next round. For the first few times, you may need to explain why a certain team's role won over another with younger students.

The role of the observer on each team is important, because it will help the team members decide the answers to the questions that follow. Observers should look for:

- Who begins the action on a team?
- Does the team decide the action as a group?
- Do individuals seek advice from each other?
- Are there team members who are resisting the group?
- How does the team handle conflict in making decisions?

After a number of rounds of this activity, ask the students to sit down and discuss what happened. The focus of the questions you would like them to dwell on should center around the role of the individual student in the process of the team's decision-making. The observers will prove to be particularly helpful here.

1. Do you feel that you took part in helping your group make a decision? If no, why not?
2. Did you find yourself changing your mind in order to avoid conflict with the others?
3. Was everyone in your group involved in the decision?

Activity 2: Tic-Tac-Toe

GOAL: To help students understand their individual behavior when they function in a class or group.

PROCEDURE: Place the chairs in the class into three rows of three chairs each. Place the chairs evenly apart. This is the "board" for the activity.

Divide the class into two teams. Ask the teams to move to opposite sides of the room. Inform the teams that you are about to play tic-tac-toe; instead of marks to indicate X's and O's, you will be asking students to play these roles. An "X" is represented by crossing arms in front of your chest. An "O" is represented by placing both hands over your head. Any team member can play any role and move on the "board" anywhere he or she would like. The team that first completes a horizontal, vertical, or diagonal line wins. The team then gains a point. All players then get up out of their chairs, and a new game is started.

The rules to this activity are few. A team member can make up his or her mind to sit anywhere on the board and assume any role. The team cannot coach or put pressure on the student to do a particular thing.

At the start of the activity, ask the teams to move to each side of the room. Ask the first player to assume a role (X or O) by moving his or her hands and then to sit in a particular chair. Ask the next team to send a player out to do the same. Continue until a team wins or until a tie occurs.

At the end of the time period, assemble the students and ask them to look closely at what happened during this activity. Typical questions to get the group discussion going could be:

1. How did you feel making your own decision?
2. Did you feel that you wanted advice from the group? Why?
3. Did you feel team pressure?
4. Is it possible that with friends you do not make a decision because of fear of the group deciding the other way?
5. Is making a decision yourself better than having the group make the decision?

Activity 3: Elephant and Giraffe

GOAL: To demonstrate how listening is important in the functioning of a group; and how helping a classmate is important and often needed.

PROCEDURE: Ask the students to assemble in a circle close enough to be able to touch, but not side by side. Ask one member to choose to be "It," and have him or her walk to the center of the circle.

"It's" role is to point to an individual in the circle and yell the word "elephant" or "giraffe." As soon as this is done, the individual must assume part of the position that is called for. In addition, those students standing on either side of this individual must also contribute part of the position. For example,

- *Elephant:* The individual pointed to must cup his or her hands and place them on the nose, so they resemble an elephant's trunk. Those students on either side must place their closest hand behind the student's ears to resemble and elephant's ears. The trio involved have five seconds to make this elephant.
- *Giraffe:* The individual pointed to must place both hands above the head. The students on either side must place their nearest hand on this student's side. This position must also be assumed in five seconds by all three students.

Ask "It" to begin, and to move the activity along fast. The only way "It" can get out of the center is by having the trio fail to complete the animal position. If any of the students chosen fails to assume the proper position, then all three individuals go into the center, and "It" can return to the circle. Once in the center, the three must allow only one member to do the pointing. The new trio is "It" until another trio fails to assume the proper position.

After a reasonable interval, ask the students to be seated, and have them answer the following questions:

1.   Were your classmates helpful?
2.   How did you feel having to rely on others to help you?
3.   Was listening to directions from the "It" hard?
4.   Were you part of a team here?

Activity 4: The Power of Words

GOAL: To describe how words can hurt and help others; to make students sensitive to these words; and to increase the use of words to help.

PROCEDURE: Put a list of statements on the board, and ask the students to describe which ones hurt another and which ones help another. Typical statements could be:

- That was stupid
- Not girls again
- That was fantastic
- I wish I could do that
- Not you again

Hold a discussion about how saying these statements could hurt or help another.

Introduce the concepts of "killer" and "stroke" statements. Killer statements are things we say to another that hurt. Stroke statements are things we say to another that helps or makes that person feel good.

Ask the students to put a killer or a stroke label in front of the statements listed above. Hold a brief discussion about how these labels fit. Now ask the students to write one statement down that they remember that another classmate said to them recently. Ask them to label it as either a killer or stroke statement. Ask students to raise their hands if the statement is a killer one; ask the students to raise their hands if the statement is a stroke one. If the majority of the statements are killer ones, you might point out to the students that killer statements are ones that are remembered the most often and for the longest time.

ACTIVITIES FOR DECEMBER

During December, the students will be asked to focus on themselves once again. Continuing a theme developed in the October activities, students will be developing their self-concept. In the activities used in December, the student will be asked to clarify his or her values. It is expected that as students begin to learn what they believe in, they will grow stronger in believing in themselves. It is this reinforced self-concept that will provide them with the self-confidence and sense of achievement to become better individuals.

Activity 1: Individual Values

GOAL: To help students identify and become aware of which values they believe are the most important, and which they believe the least important.

PROCEDURE: Distribute Form 4-1. Ask the students to place an "L" next to the values they like in themselves, and a "D" next to those they dislike.

Ask the students to pick one close friend and to choose a value they like most about this friend. Then ask them to pick a value they like least about this friend. Discuss with the students the differences and similarities between themselves and their friends.

VALUES DISPLAY

Place an "L" next to the values that you like about yourself, and a "D" next to the values that you do not like about yourself.

_____	Loyal	_____	Tough
_____	Selfish	_____	Flirty
_____	Loving	_____	Helpful
_____	Honest	_____	Friendly
_____	Fair	_____	Unique
_____	Nice	_____	Good
_____	Fool	_____	Poor
_____	Cute	_____	Smart
_____	Rich	_____	
_____	Expert	_____	
_____	Perfect	_____	

Form 4-1

Activity 2: Name Values

GOAL: To help students choose values to describe themselves to others.

PROCEDURE: Distribute name tags or stickers to students. Ask each student to write his or her name in such a manner that the letters are evenly spaced across the tag.

Ask the students to think of positive adjectives that begin with each letter of their name and which they feel describes themselves well. The use of a dictionary may be helpful here. Ask the students to write these adjectives on the name sticker as shown below:

S	U	E
w	n	n
e	i	e
e	q	r
t	u	g
	e	e
		t
		i
		c

The students should place the tags on their clothing and circulate around the room for everyone to view. If, for some reason, a student cannot think of an adjective that fits, then ask other students to help fill in the missing slot for that person's name.

If time permits, the class could hold a discussion on this activity. Have students ask each other why he or she chose a particular adjective over another.

Activity 3: Social Barometer

GOAL: To help students identify and express their opinion about a particular issue.

PROCEDURE: The barometer to be used needs to be drawn on a large sheet of rolled paper. If paper is not available, then mark off the barometer with tape on the floor. Figure 4-1 shows a sample barometer.

Ask the students to stand at the zero point. Describe how a barometer works. If the mood or feeling about something is positive, then the student moves to the positive side of the barometer. If the mood or feeling is negative, then the student moves to the negative side. If someone feels very strongly about an issue, then that student moves to the extreme end of the barometer. If there is no opinion, then the person stays at zero.

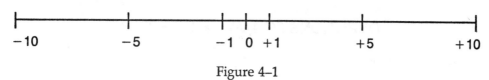

Figure 4–1

Pick a fun issue at first to illustrate how this works. For example, call out, "Hot dogs." All students who absolutely love hot dogs should move to the +10 area. Those who hate hot dogs would move to the −10 area, and those who have mild opinions would move to the halfway points, +5 or −5. Those who have never eaten a hot dog would remain at zero.

Next, call out certain issues and ask the students to move quickly up and down the barometer. Sample issues are mom, dad, English, food, police, drugs, TV, school rules, the principal, summer vacation, brothers, and sisters. There should be no time to talk or to make comments about who goes where and with whom.

You should make mental notes of what is happening to individuals in the group as they move about: Who likes to go in different directions? Who changed their minds when they noted the group going in opposite directions? Who cannot make up their minds? Who is most negative or most positive?

Activity 4: Value Interview

GOAL: To help students form judgments about issues and to communicate these judgments to others.

PROCEDURE: Write the following rules on the chalkboard:

1.   Only you and your partner will know the answer.
2.   If you ask your partner a question, he or she has the right to ask you the same question.
3.   You may decline to answer any question.

Inform the students that the interview worksheet (see Form 4-2) will be distributed to each of them. Ask the students to form pairs. Remind the students that their opinions are to remain in the partnership and that everything is confidential.

Then ask the students to interview each other. Each person should have enough time so that the partner can ask further questions if necessary.

Activity 5: Future Values

GOAL: To help students form value judgments about what they think will be important to them in the future.

QUESTIONS FOR VALUE INTERVIEW

1. How do you feel today?

2. Do you care for your class?

3. Do you share with others?

4. How do you feel when someone does not listen when you talk?

5. What do you think about the rules here?

6. What do you do when you have a problem?

7. What turns you off the fastest?

8. What do you wish others here knew about you?

© 1988 by The Center for Applied Research in Education

Form 4-2

PROCEDURE: Distribute the worksheet given in Form 4-3. Ask the students to choose a certain number of values (for example, five, three, or two) and have them rank-order their future importance in their lives.

ACTIVITIES FOR JANUARY

In today's world, it is critical that students learn how to survive socially. It is essential that students be taught some of the social skills necessary to deal with the many pressures and demands that are part of living. The activities for January focus on teaching skills not normally taught in school. Specific objectives include how to identify stress, how to deal with it, how to handle issues related to death and dying, how to become aware of one's rights, and skill-training. Most of this month's activities will require more than one class period to accomplish.

Activity 1: Identifying Stress

GOAL: To show students how to identify stressful situations; how to measure the intensity of the stress; and how to deal with the stress.

PROCEDURE: The object here is to teach students how stress works. One method is to compare stress to the physical exhaustion that can happen to one's muscles if they are used too long and too intensely. Ask the students to clench their fists very tightly and to hold this position for a full ten seconds. At about the sixth second, ask students to be aware of the intense pressure and strain that is starting to occur in the muscles of their fists and arms. At the tenth-second mark, ask students to release their fists. Mention to them how much better and relaxed they now feel.

What they just experienced was physical stress. Now draw the comparison between physical and emotional stresses. While it is easy to show physical stress—you just did, it is not as easy to show emotional stress. One of the best ways to describe emotional stress is to compare it to the speedometer in a car. Figure 4-2 could be drawn on the chalkboard to demonstrate emotional stress.

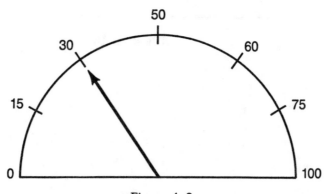

Figure 4–2

FUTURE VALUES WORKSHEET

What do you want most from life? Choose _____ from the list below, and number them in order of importance, with "1" being the most important.

_____ a job

_____ a car

_____ travel

_____ a personality

_____ a friend

_____ money

_____ love

_____ children

_____ to be famous

_____ to do something challenging

_____ to move to another country

_____ an education

_____ a spouse

Form 4-3

The 0 level indicates little or no stress present. The 50-point level indicates high stress, and the 100-point level indicates stress at the extreme level of emotional breakdown. The speedometer needle will go up or down during the course of a day, adjusting to the stressful events. The danger, like that of driving too fast, is having one's stress indicator over 50 for most of the day. The body has great difficulty handling such stress, and mood changes result in the individual.

Inform the students that there are three causes of emotional stress: (1) from threats, (2) from frustration, and (3) from conflict. Ask the students to provide examples of each. Hopefully, they will do so from their own lives. If not, then you will need to provide examples that fit the age and maturity of your students. Listed below are three examples for emotionally-disturbed middle-school-aged students:

1. *From threats:* The town bully has told you that he is going to be waiting for you when you get off the bus after school today.
2. *From frustration:* The school principal has told you that you must stay after school in detention if you are in the hall without a pass. However, you cannot find the pass you had.
3. *From conflict:* Your teacher has told you that she is going to call your mother because you refuse to follow directions.

With stress that comes with any of the above examples, there is a dramatic change in the body's chemistry. Your heart rate and pulse rate increase, and extra chemicals are pumped into the bloodstream. As a result, your mood changes. Some people become more excited, depressed, angry, or withdrawn. You should ask students if they know how they react to emotional stress. Do any of the above mood changes characterize them? If they do not know, inform them that one of the activity's objectives is to help them learn about how they handle stress.

For example, Craig has been told by his father that, if he ever is seen in the company of Jim, he will suffer severe punishment. Craig's father has hit him in the past, and so Craig is afraid of his father. Craig thought he was safe when he and Jim went to the local store on the far side of the town. However, as the two were leaving the store, Craig's father happened to be driving by in his pickup truck. He slowed down just enough to yell to Craig that he was going to get it tonight when he got home.

Craig was relaxing with his friend Jim and had little or no stress. His stress needle was at zero. As soon as his father yelled at him, Craig's stress needle went to 80. Since it would be four hours before his father came home, Craig would now worry about going home for four hours. During this time, Craig's stress needle stayed at 80. Since he was well over the 50 point mark and into the danger zone, and since this level held for a long period of time, Craig showed signs of wear. His reaction to this threat from his father was to become angry. On the way home, Craig let air out of a car's tire and threw a soda can at a boy passing on a bike. Clearly, Craig was having difficulty handling this emotional stress.

The next step in this activity is for the students to look at their own stress speedometer and try to determine at what level their own stress needle would record particular events. Spend some time having the students discuss their reactions to the stress chart.

VARIATION: Another variation associated with this activity is to have a stress indicator similar to the one shown in Figure 4-2 posted in your class. At any time of the day, you could invite students to move the stress needle to whatever mark they feel is appropriate for them.

Activity 2: Dealing with Stress

GOAL: To teach students three ways to deal with stress.

PROCEDURE: Now that the students have been able to identify stress, it is time to teach them ways to deal with it. There are many books on this subject, and you may want to use other stress-reduction methods. Three are given here to start you off.

1. *Progressive Relaxation:* This method involves a series of muscle relaxation activities that are designed to start at the foot muscles and to move up the body until the head muscles are relaxed. A reference book that contains a record you could use to initiate this relaxation, if you feel uneasy doing it yourself, is *Progressive Relaxation Training* by Douglas Berstein and Thomas Borkovec (Champaign, IL: Research Press, 1973).

Teaching the method to students will enable them to use it at home when they feel their stress indicator going over the 50-point mark.

Basically, tell the student, "Find a comfortable chair or even lie on the floor. Close your eyes and concentrate on the directions given. First, start by tightening the muscles in the left foot and holding this position until the strain is felt. After a few seconds, lessen the tightness and feel the relaxation in the foot muscle. Repeat the procedure. Again, concentrate on how the relaxed muscle feels. Proceed to tighten the calf, then the leg muscles. Next, think of your right foot, calf, and leg, repeat muscle tension, and then release the muscles. Then move to the buttocks and the back, the stomach, the chest, the neck, the cheek, the nose, and the forehead muscles. With each muscle, first tighten it, and then release it to feel the relaxation set in. At the end of this exercise, you should feel very relaxed, concentrating on the muscle relaxation over the entire body. When ready, open your eyes, and get up."

2. *Body Bends:* Have the students stand with their feet together. Ask them to bend at the waist with their arms extended downward pointing at the floor. The students need not touch their toes. Tell the students to hold this position for a few seconds and then gradually straighten up, blowing air out of their noses as they

rise. Ask the students to concentrate on how relaxed this position makes them feel. Ask them to repeat this exercise and have them concentrate on how relaxed their bodies feel.

3. *Talk It Out:* The easiest—yet difficult to initiate— method of releasing stress is to have the students talk it out with someone that they can trust. Many students find that talking it out can be very difficult. It is important you tell these students that it is OK to talk about things that may be bothering them. Inform them that talking is one way of dealing with the issues. Ideally, one or two adults in the school building should be available, with whom students can talk about their personal problems. Invite these adults into your room to introduce themselves. Encourage them to come by the class often just to say hello. Ask the students if they could identify one friend with whom they could talk to about problems. Next month, students will be trained in how to listen and help each other.

An activity that can be of assistance in structuring talking-it-out involves the use of the Personal Stress Chart. (See Form 4-4.) Pass out this chart to all members of the class. Ask the students to fill in the chart, and to add any items that may be of interest to them. Once the students have completed the chart, note for yourself those areas that are marked with a 50+ stress level. At some later date, you may want to engage these students in a conversation about what is bothering them.

Activity 3: Living with Dying

GOAL: To help students deal with the issues of death, dying, and the loss of a close person.

PROCEDURE: This activity will cause the stress levels of your students to go up. Tell them that this is normal and that once you get into the activity, this stress will drop, and they will be able to deal with the subject.

You will find various levels of maturity in your class about the fear of death. You will also find that similar concerns arise when students' friends and relatives go to the hospital for an operation, or when these individuals have been hospitalized for a long time. Usually, one or two of the students have had some experience with a relative dying, so there will be some who can draw from personal experience.

For younger children, you may need to adapt your talk about the issue of death by talking about the death of a pet. The same feelings are present as when you talk to an older student about the death of a person.

It has been our experience to structure this activity very closely. A film strip dealing with this matter is an excellent reference point from which good discussions develop. There are many on the commercial market, but one that is recommended is, *"Living With Dying, Parts I and II."* It is distributed by Sunburst Communication (101 Castleton Avenue, Pleasantville, New York 10570).

PERSONAL STRESS CHART

List the amount of stress (0-100) you think each of the situations below would cause you.

_____ Seeing the principal coming toward you

_____ Failing a course

_____ Knowing your teacher will be calling your parent

_____ Having your pet die

_____ Thinking of summer vacation

_____ _____

_____ _____

_____ _____

_____ _____

_____ _____

_____ _____

_____ _____

_____ _____

_____ _____

Form 4-4

This filmstrip deals with a teenager talking about her own feelings of having a terminal disease. The scenes in the hospital are quite realistic, and the questions at the end of each section lead to excellent discussions.

You will find that the activity prepares students to deal with a part of life. You will probably have previous students come back to you and relate how the discussions helped them deal with a particular tragedy.

Activity 4: Social-Skills Training

GOAL: To reinforce specific social skills in students.

PROCEDURE: Teaching social skills to students can be a very frustrating task. One method of accomplishing this task is to incorporate the skills acquisition into existing board game activities. In this way, students learn the skills and, at the same time, enjoy a game of mutual cooperative interaction. For many special education students, the task of just participating in a board game is a success task, in and of itself. There are many skills associated with a board game that by themselves are important, including following rules, patience, postponing one's impulses, working as a team, and handling pressure.

Below are two different methods of teaching additional social skills using traditional board games. The games can be purchased commercially.

1. *Connect Four:* This game is good for mentally retarded students. The object of the game is to put the checkers into a vertical tray, so that one's particular color (red or black) scores four in a row either vertically, horizontally, or diagonally.

2. *UNO:* This game is good for older students, because it involves some decision-making skills. Students are dealt cards that have colored numbers on the reverse side. The students must follow the number or color sequence in playing their cards. There are a number of switch and trick cards that make the game interesting. The winner is the first player that gets rid of all his or her cards.

With both games, a modified card deck should be developed. For the Connect Four game, a student must successfully answer a question the particular card poses before he or she gets to place a checker. Failure to answer the card correctly means a loss of a turn. The Uno game uses a similar format. Before a student can place a card, the question from the teacher-developed card deck must be answered.

On each card (index cards will do), write a particular social situation that requires a particular appropriate social response. You, as the teacher, will be the judge regarding whether or not the answer to the particular question is appropriate. You may need to rehearse the social skills before the game is played. The best part of the game is the constant repetition. With time and with the same social skills being emphasized, the students will eventually learn aspects of how to cope in social situations. The repetition becomes reinforcing.

The teacher should choose which social skills need to be written on the game cards. These skills can be quite specific and catered to the class needs. A few suggestions are listed here.

Skill	*Question*
1. Compliment another	1. Tell a person one thing you like about him or her.
2. Criticism	2. Tell a person one thing you do not like about him or her.
3. Politeness	3. State four appropriate things, to say to people (e.g., please, excuse me, thank you, you are welcome).
4. Questioning	4. Ask for advice about an issue.
5. Social interaction	5. State one way to start a conversation.
6. Social confrontation	6. State how you feel about an issue.

Activity 5: Know Your Rights

GOAL: To inform students of their rights under the law.

PROCEDURE: For this activity, it might be a good idea to call in some outside experts to speak to the class. Essentially, the goal of this activity is the imparting of information about the law, one's rights, and where one can get help.

Depending on the age of your students, you will have to adjust the topics covered. Certainly, issues arising from divorce, child abuse, neglect, and juvenile law are topics that could be developed. Most states and large cities have departments in juvenile law, and officials are available to speak to classes. The local police should be asked to talk about the law as it relates to students. Perhaps, the school principal could be asked to speak about school rules and regulations. A local lawyer could address the class about how a lawyer could be of assistance. Child-advocate agencies usually have speakers available to visit school classes. You may also want to initiate a visit to a local courthouse to view a trial in session. You may wish to write to the administrative judge to make an appointment for the class to visit the court. In some cases, the judge will be available to talk to the class about the case and answer questions from the students.

ACTIVITIES FOR FEBRUARY

The activities for February will teach students how to communicate more effectively. These skills are essential if students are to be effective in their everyday lives. The lack of any one of them inhibits a student's ability to grow personally and academically. These activities are sequenced, so that they build on each other. Specific objectives to be covered are observation skills, trust, communication, and listening.

Activity 1: Observation Power

GOAL: To help students gain an understanding of how perception can be very individualistic and therefore limiting.

PROCEDURE: It is best to divide the class into small groups. Each group will take a walk around the school in the company of an adult. The goal of the group is to remember as many things they see as possible. The adult will take notes of particular things seen along the way, and the notes can be used as a basis for forming questions later. Explain to the students that nothing dramatic is going to be seen. They will see the normal things that go on in a school.

Once back in the room, question the students and have them write their answers on a sheet of paper. Remind them that you will be asking them to recall things that they saw on the walk. Typical questions are the following:

- What color was the suit the principal was wearing?
- Who walked between the group on the second floor?
- Where was the spill of water?
- What color was the car that went by us in the parking lot?

Once this exercise is completed, tell the students the right answers. Ask them to tally up their correct responses and to let you know who was the most observant. Avoid questions of opinion, such as, "Which class was the noisiest?"

A general discussion can now follow about the power of observation. Usually, so much is happening in a school building that no one can see it all. Therefore, keep reminding students that what they have observed about an event may not be the only thing that was happening. Others may have seen other things about those events that are just as valid. Relate this activity to examples from events in students' lives. Were observations difficult to make? Did other observers see these same events differently?

Activity 2: Trust Walks

GOAL: To demonstrate how communication can be improved.

PROCEDURE: A maze needs to be built in the class for this activity. Arrange the chairs, desks, and other class items to construct a simple maze through which a student will walk. Have the student perform a simple task when he or she reaches the end of the maze. For example, have the students draw a hand on the board about the size of a human hand. Once the student reaches the end of the maze, he or she needs to place his or her hand inside the drawn hand. This may seem simple, but the hard part is that the student does these tasks blindfolded.

Ask for a volunteer to leave the room while the maze is built. Blindfold the student. Once the student enters the room, you need to give some simple directions. You should inform the student that there is a maze of chairs and desks in front of him or her and that he or she will be directed through the maze by the students. One command will be given at a time. At the end of the maze, the student will be asked to complete a task. Assure the student that you will not let anything dangerous happen and that you are in complete control of the event.

Each class student is to give a command. For example, a student may say to the walker, "make a ninety-degree turn to the right." The next student may say, "Take four small steps forward." Continue having the class taking turns until the student completes the maze and does the task at the end. Ask the student to take off his or her blindfold. Hold a class discussion now about what happened. Ask the student who he or she trusted the most, and why. Ask about the commands. Were they relevant and accurate? How did the experience feel? Then ask the class if anyone had difficulty figuring out how to give an accurate command.

Explain that the only successful way to help a fellow student through this activity is to view the situation through his or her eyes. Explain this statement as what communication is all about—trying to understand another's view of the situation. You may wish to relate this activity to the last activity on observation power. By relating the two activities, you reinforce the idea that one's perception of an event is limited and, that to truly understand the event, one needs to understand how another views the situation.

This activity can be done many times. The maze will need to be redrawn each time and a new volunteer asked to leave the room.

Activity 3: Communication

GOAL: To show students how communication between two people can be helpful or damaging depending on the methods used.

PROCEDURE: Ask each student to take out a sheet of paper. Ask for a volunteer to stand before the class and describe something. Inform the class that they are not to ask questions, but to simply draw what the volunteer asks them to draw. There must be silence here.

Hand the volunteer a drawing (see Form 4-5). Turn the volunteer around so the class cannot see his or her face. The volunteer can give as many commands as he or she likes to get the job done. After a brief period, stop the event, and ask the volunteer to show the class the drawing that is being attempted by the class.

Now ask for a second volunteer. This person will also describe a drawing (see Form 4- 6), but this time the volunteer may face the class and answer any questions. After a period of time during which the class has been drawing the diagram, ask the class and volunteer to stop. Ask the volunteer to show the drawing to the class.

Now ask the students to spend time describing the differences between the two events. Which was easier and produced the better results? Does the ability to ask questions help in the process? Which form of communication do they prefer?

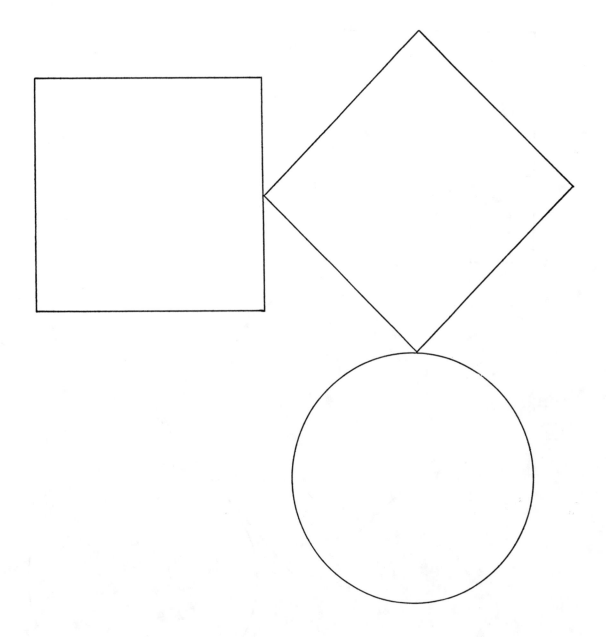

Form 4-5

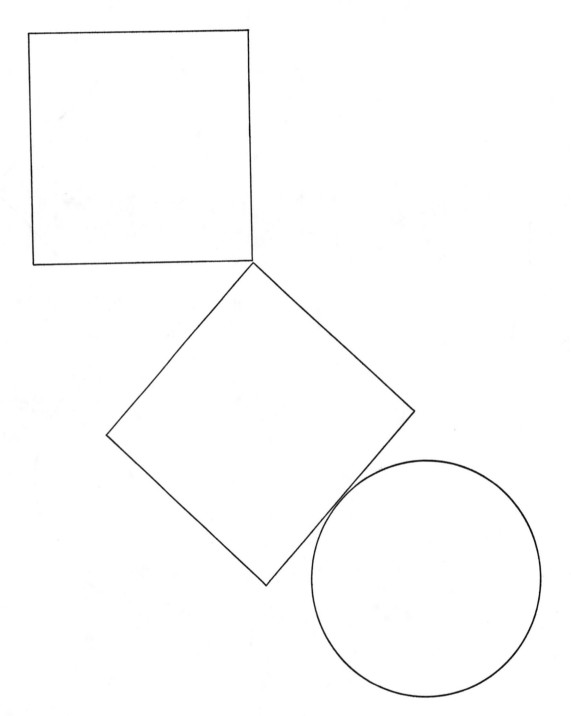

Form 4-6

150

Ask the students which form of communication they see in the school. Are students given a chance to ask questions? If yes, how does that help or hinder communication? If no, how does that help or hinder communication? Can the students think of any other places where these two different forms of communication may or may not exist?

Activity 4: Masking-Tape Game

GOAL: To demonstrate how communication with others affects our feelings.

PROCEDURE: Cut pieces of masking tape about 4 inches long, so that there is one piece for each class member. On each piece, write some instructions, such as:

- Ignore me.
- Listen to me.
- Tell me I'm right.
- Tell me I'm wrong.
- Praise me.
- Ridicule me.

Place the masking tape on each student's forehead so that the student cannot see the role he or she will be playing.

Now introduce a topic for discussion; for example, school should not be mandatory. Tell the class that they have about five minutes to discuss this issue. Everyone should be able to see everyone else's masking tape. Instruct the class to do to the student what the masking tape says. If the topic does not generate enough discussion, introduce a new one. At the end of the discussion, ask the students to guess what role they were playing. Ask them to remove their tape to verify this guess.

The discussion that follows this activity should focus on the feelings one has, as others try to communicate with us. Depending on how people treat us by their communications, we may either feel good or bad. A good question to generate is, "Are our feelings about ourselves dependent on how others interact with us?"

Activity 5: Listening

GOAL: To teach students how to listen.

PROCEDURE: Divide the class into groups of three students each. Ask one student to become the speaker, one the listener, and one the observer. Remind the students that each will get a chance to assume the other roles. Ask the speaker to talk for one minute about a preselected topic. An example might be; "My favorite food." The role of the listener is to try to remember the content of what the speaker says. After a minute, the speaker will stop, and the listener must repeat back as much accurate feedback as possible.

The role of the observer is to rate (excellent, good, poor) the listener on how well he or she listened.

Then ask the students to switch roles, so that each student gets to play each role.

At the end of the session, hold a discussion on how hard it is to listen. Remind the students that, to be a good listener, one really needs to concentrate.

ACTIVITIES FOR MARCH

The activities for this month will be used to teach students to communicate more about themselves to each other. The objective for this month is to have the students get to know each other, so they will get to understand each other better. Not only will class activities be completed in a more cooperative way but also the academic work of the class should improve. Students will not spend time fighting among themselves nor diverting energy from academic tasks to solve personality misunderstandings in the class. At the end of the month, students will be given the opportunity to put their knowledge of each other to use by cooperating in a class project.

Activity 1: Mixed Bag

GOAL: To demonstrate to students a method for improving understanding in a class.

PROCEDURE: For this activity, you will need plenty of old magazines and scissors for the students to use. Each student will also need a small paper bag. Inform the students that it will take a class period to find pictures, words, or drawings in various magazines that they feel describe them. They are to tape, onto the outside of the bag, those pictures that they feel describe what others know about themselves. This category can be referred to as, "What others and I know about myself." Inside the bag, students are to place objects or pictures that they feel describes what no one in the class knows about them. This category can be referred to as, "What I know about myself, but others do not."

Take some time for this activity to be completed. Assure the students that those items inside the bag are their confidential information. No one will be asked to reveal this information against his or her wishes.

Divide the class into groups of two once the activity is finished. Ask the students to describe the items they have on the outside of their bag to their partner. The partner has a right to ask questions about these items.

Once this phase is completed, inform the students that they can share one item that is inside their bag if they wish. However, inform them that this activity is optional; the information is to be shared only with a partner, not with the entire class.

The objective of this lesson is to inform students that communication can be improved if the other understands you better. A way of improving communication is to share information about yourself.

Activity 2: Talk-Behind-Your-Back

GOAL: To help students learn what others think of them.

PROCEDURE: This is a relatively easy activity to organize, but a somewhat risky one to operate. Let us take the easy part first. Ask for a volunteer to sit with his or her back to the class. Explain to the class that the object of this activity is for the students to talk about the student who is sitting. The student sitting down may not comment on anything said, but should just listen. Explain to the sitting student that just listening will be difficult, but that it is important for him or her to hear everything said.

Now, let's tackle the hard part. Depending on the composition of your class, you will need to give different types of directions to the students who will be talking. For example, you may ask younger children or children who have limited verbal ability to say just one or two things about the person sitting down. Give one of the students a specific number of things to say: "Now Bob, I want you to say two things about Elizabeth that would describe her." Or, you can play with variations on this theme. Suggest that a stranger is visiting your school and has asked that the sitting student be described by at least two words. For sitting students who are impulsive and behavior problems, you may suggest that the comments of the class be only positive in nature. For other sitting students, you will want to take precautions to avoid having the class group "dump" on them.

In general, however, encourage the class to talk about the sitting student by commenting on what each has said about him or her. People need not agree with each other. The sitting student should hear a running discussion of others talking about him or her.

Once the first volunteer has finished, then ask for another to proceed to the chair. The class now talks about this student. Continue until all have had a turn. You should include yourself in this as well.

At the end of the activity, draw the class together and hold a general discussion on what happened. Ask if anyone learned something new about themselves. Ask students if they heard something they liked or disliked. Ask them how they felt going through this activity.

Activity 3: Share a Concern

GOAL: To allow students to help each other with problems.

PROCEDURE: For this activity, ask each student to write a concern or problem they may be having. The problem may be one at home, in the community, in school, or with a friend. Ask them to fold the sheet of paper, and place the concern in a box. Advise them that these concerns will be read out loud and not to put their names on the paper. Stress the confidentiality of the matter. You could even introduce the activity as a form of writing a "Dear Abby" letter.

Collect all the concerns, and then ask each student to draw out a concern and unfold the paper. If a student draws a concern that he or she wrote, the student has the option of putting it back in the box and drawing another one.

One at a time, each student should now read the concern that he or she has drawn. The rest of the students should give advice to help resolve this concern. You will find, as you do this activity, that many students provide some very good advice for problem resolution. Some students speak from experience, and others know students who have had similar problems. Many ideas are generated in this type of format. You should direct the activity to ensure that the confidentiality of the writer is protected. Sometimes, a student will volunteer that the concern being read is his or hers, but do not encourage this type of volunteerism. When you feel the discussion about a particular concern has naturally finished, then move on to the next student.

Activity 4: Class Project

GOAL: To give the students an opportunity to work together on a common task.

PROCEDURE: Announce to the class that they need to choose a class project that they can all work on. This project should be one that they feel they all can benefit from, as well as one that will provide a service to the school or community. The scope of the project will vary depending on the age and ability of your students. If possible, first allow the students to brainstorm ideas, and discuss ways of accomplishing each project. Then, have them vote on which project they feel best represents the class wishes. The time spent in the project need not be extensive. (There is an activity in May which incorporates class project activities that could be more time consuming.) At this point, suggest that the project that is selected be one that can be completed in a week.

Some ideas for a project are the following ones:

- Writing letters to students in other schools/states/countries
- Cleaning up a street, a park, or a stream of trash and garbage
- Building a plant holder for the school's lobby
- Planting flowers around the school or in a town park
- Visiting a nursing home, a hospital, or a day-care center
- Publishing a small newspaper of school news, poems, etc.

- Asking the school secretary if they can help with any filing, cleaning, or collating
- Designing and painting a large mural for the cafeteria wall.

With any activity chosen, it is important to remember that the class be involved together in its inception, work, and results. Everyone should do something. Once the project is completed, then plan a ceremony to dedicate it or to praise its completion. Encourage the principal to become involved in honoring the students. Post a sign to announce who did what on the project. The students should feel like team members and be very proud of the successful completion of the project.

ACTIVITIES FOR APRIL

The April activities are devoted to looking at group processes, and how these processes effect the behavior of the individual. Students should know and trust each other well enough by now, so that they should be ready to look at how the class functions as a group. It is hoped that, as they look at themselves, they might also look at other groups in the school and community to which they belong. During this month, students will specifically learn how they function in groups, how group pressure works, and what roles individuals play in groups.

Activity 1: Break In/Break Out

GOAL: To provide students with the feelings associated with belonging to and entering a group.

PROCEDURE: Ask for a volunteer to walk off to the side of the class. Assemble the rest of the class in a tight circle. Inform the circle of students that they must make it difficult for the volunteer to enter the group. The volunteer is told that his or her task is to try to break into the group. Time this activity for just a few minutes. Advise against rough play or physical abuse. Usually, the students in the circle join arms when the outsider tries to break in. Sometimes, you will find that a student is capable of negotiating his or her way into the group. Repeat this experience a number of times with different students.
    At this point, hold a general discussion about how the students felt about the activity. How did it feel to be left out, to be rejected, and to fight to get in? How did it feel to hold someone out of the group. Did it matter if this person was a friend? Draw parallels to students' experiences of trying to get into a certain clique, lunch table, bus seat, or class. Can similar feelings be identified in these circumstances?

VARIATION: An alternative form of the activity is to have a volunteer try to break out of a group. In a similar fashion, draw inferences to other group experiences a student may find in school or in the community.

Activity 2: What Do You Mean?

GOAL: To help students gain some clarification about how others in the class think of them.

PROCEDURE: This activity can be a lot of fun, and students can gain insight. Divide the class into pairs. Ask each student to write something about the other to describe that person. The sentence should begin with: "I think you are ?????."

Once the students have completed one sentence, they should decide on who is going to go first. The student who goes first reads the sentence to the other. The next student must seek clarification of this statement by asking a number of "do you mean" questions. For example:

- Jim writes of Frank: I think you are *smart*.
- Frank responds: "By *smart*, do you mean that I get A's?"
- Jim answers: "Yes."
- Frank asks: "By *smart*, do you mean that I study hard?"

In other words, the student is getting more information about what his or her partner said by asking "do you mean" questions. A good rule of thumb is for the student to ask this question twice. Once the first two students have completed the activity, ask the students to reform and group themselves for another round of the activity

Activity 3: Classroom Move

GOAL: To give students an opportunity to view how each individual operates in a group.

PROCEDURE: It is best to divide the class into small groups of no more than five students. Assign the class members the task of deciding where in the building they would like to move their classroom. They must follow the rules listed below and they must reach a common agreement:

1. The room must be a classroom presently used in the building.
2. The room must be large enough to hold the entire class.
3. They must decide to move to another room.
4. The time limit for this activity will be 15 minutes.

During the class discussions, you should observe the various roles each student plays in the group's discussion. Some points to note are:

1. Who was the leader? How was this evident, and did the leadership change?

2. Did the students listen to each other, or was everyone trying to talk at once?

3. How did the group deal with an individual or individuals who did not agree with the solution of the majority?

4. Would you describe the tone of the discussions as friendly, loud, nonfriendly, quiet, confused, or orderly?

5. Did anything happen in the group that was unique, and why?

Activity 4: Group Observation

GOAL: To give students a real experience to use observations skills to determine the roles people play in a group.

PROCEDURE: Divide the class into small working groups. The size of the group should be dependent on the maturity of the individuals. It is suggested that the groups be kept small. For younger children, you might have four students to a group; for older students, no more than two.

The group's task is to observe students in the school in natural settings, and to record the various behaviors of the students. The students are to use their new knowledge of the roles individuals play in a group to complete this task. An observation record (see Form 4-7) will give the activity some more structure.

Some suggested places for students to observe would be the school library, cafeteria, gym, outdoor meeting areas, or the bus. Anyplace where large numbers of other students gather is appropriate.

Once the students have completed the task of observing, it is suggested that they report to the class about what they saw. Names of the students involved in the observation can be deleted, so that the students can concentrate on the information about group roles rather than on the personalities of those involved. Generally, these group discussions can be very stimulating, for they enable students to become more aware of the various group activities operating in the building.

After about five minutes, ask the groups to stop their discussions. Ask for a member of the group to be a spokesperson and to report the group's answer to the problem of where the class should move. At this point, you should inform the group that, as they were talking, you were moving about and recording the behavior of group members. You should let the individual students know what roles you saw them play. It is best to give a description of the role rather than just a label. For example, rather than saying, "Mary, you were a real leader here," you might say, "Mary, you showed leadership skills when you asked the group to stop talking to each other, and to start listening to each other."

Let the students know that there are no right or wrong roles for students to play in the group. All roles are important and needed. In addition to the informa-

OBSERVATION RECORD

1. Where did this group meet?

2. What was the group talking about?

3. Did everyone agree?

4. How did the group deal with the person who disagreed?

5. Which roles (leader, follower, joker, nonparticipator, blocker, ally, aggressor, other) were acted in the group?

6. How did the leader lead the group?

7. Which role helped the group?

Form 4-7

tion you recorded for the above questions, you might also point out other roles students played: e.g., blocker, dominator, joker, non-participator, or confronter.

Once you have given your observations, ask the group of students for theirs. Ask if they saw any roles being played. Ask how they felt about the role that they played.

For younger children, you could adapt this activity to ask them to agree on a color that they would like their classroom painted. If students have limited verbal ability, you could ask them to work together on a simple puzzle, or to engage in some other nonverbal activity that would reveal roles in a group setting.

ACTIVITIES FOR MAY

All of the activities for May are designed to allow students to integrate the many skills they have already learned in this chapter. Essentially, the students will be given tasks to complete as a group. To complete these tasks successfully, the students will need to rely on the many skills that they learned over the course of the school year. Such skills as those relating to interpersonal relationships, communications, values, and group process will be needed to problem-solve each task. In addition, an integrated positive self-concept, developed earlier in this chapter's activities, will be needed to ensure that a student can successfully compete in the tasks. Because of the time factor, you may finish only one or two of these activities.

Activity 1: Field Trip

GOAL: To provide students with a challenging task; and to promote a better understanding of themselves.

PROCEDURE: This activity may seem like something you have done many times before; however, there is a twist this time. It is suggested that the entire class be given the task of deciding where to go on a field trip—within reason, of course. This type of responsibility demands that the students focus in agreeing on something that could benefit all of them.

You could give students some guidelines if you feel that the group needs to be directed and given some realistic limitations. Generally, however, it is best that the class itself be allowed to go through the decision-making process, even though there may be some fantastic suggestions offered first. The group process itself should provide some realism to the event. For example, if the group initially decides to go to another state for the trip, it may conclude that the whole idea is impractical once it looks at costs and transportation.

Some general topics to focus on are the following:

- A place to visit
- How to get there
- When to go

- What to bring
- Who should go
- Cost

You should have a chance to comment on the various dynamics that take place during the many discussions that the class will have as it tries to solve these problems. Mention listening problems, interpersonal communication deficits, group process, and group roles that are being played. The students will use all of this information as feedback for the task that they are trying to solve. They will learn the many lessons of this chapter as they do so.

Activity 2: Community Service Project

GOAL: To allow students to give back to their community something of themselves in exchange for all that the community has done for them.

PROCEDURE: This project is somewhat different from the project the class may have completed in March. This project should be more extensive and perhaps even planned by the class itself. To complete this activity, some time will be needed away from the school. The class should work on this project as a unit, utilizing the many skills that it has learned over the course of the year to complete the task successfully.

First start with the class brainstorming ideas for a project. A discussion of the ideas should follow with closure and agreement on one single project. It may be necessary for the class to appoint a few students to act as spokespeople, and to have them discuss the leads with the school principal. The town or city recreation, police, or public works departments may be contacted to elicit their cooperation.

Suggested projects include:

- Spring clean up of the park, school property, or playing fields
- Laying out of the playing fields with chalk lines, and erecting the goal posts and goal nets
- Painting of town or city park benches
- Helping in the local historical society
- Planning and executing a play activity for the recreation department or for a local kindergarten class

Throughout the time the class is involved in these projects, the teacher should offer feedback to the students. Point out the various roles the students are playing. Indicate communication problems and communication successes. In general, try to help the students feel that the task is being completed because the class is working together as a unit.

Activity 3: Plant Sale

GOAL: To demonstrate to students how they can function together as a group to accomplish a specific task.

PROCEDURE: This activity can be successfully completed in the school building. The goal is to sell plants to the teachers, the PTA, and to other students. Usually garden plants are being planted this time of year in many parts of the country, so these would be ideal items to focus a class activity around.

You could start this activity early in the school year by asking the students to buy seeds from companies through the mail. Planting the seeds and helping them to grow in the classroom is an ideal project for many students. Once the plants are large enough and the planting time ideal, the class could organize a sale. This activity will help students learn the basics of business as well. The students will need to establish a common selling price that is adjusted so that the class can make a profit. Each student should be allowed to sell to customers. Perhaps by assigning certain plants to different students, the teacher could ensure that each student has a fair chance of making a profit. You might also want to role-play a typical customer-student encounter so that students are comfortable with the interpersonal exchange that will take place. Advertising should also be included in the activities associated with this project. If growing plants from seeds is a problem, the teacher could buy plants from a local nursery and have the students resell them to the customers at the school for a profit. Remind students that all profits go to the class treasury. This money will be applied to the class for a party at the end of the school year.

Activity 4: Jog-a-Thon

GOAL: To help students organize a fund-raising activity and, at the same time, have fun.

PROCEDURE: There may be an activity you would like to participate in with your students, but you do not have sufficient funds to cover the expenses. If you are looking for a way for the class to raise money and would still like to keep the theme for this month's activities, then a jog-a-thon may be a way to do both. A jog-a-thon can raise a great deal of money; at the same time, it can provide the class with an activity that demands group participation, group communication, and group decision-making.

The first task is for the class to decide how many laps around the track it thinks each student can run. Another task, if the class cannot solve the first, is to decide how long a time the class should jog. The class should not be looking for endurance runs, but for a moderate amount of time. Class members should get tired, but not exhausted, from the run. For secondary students, it may be a 30-

minute jog for everyone around the track. For primary-level students, a shorter period of time is necessary.

Once the class has decided on the first task, it then needs to decide on how much money it would like to collect for every lap or for every minute that it jogs around the track.

The third task is to find sponsors for this jog-a-thon. Some publicity will be needed to encourage people to pledge money for this fund raiser. It might be a good idea to tell people directly what this jog-a-thon money will be used for. An example of a sales pitch might be: "Would you like to pledge a nickel a lap for every lap I will run. The money collected will be used for a class trip to Boston this year." The date of the jog-a-thon could be one day or may even be stretched over a week's time to allow every special-education-student time to jog.

After the jog, students will need to collect money. Ask them to be persistent in collecting their pledges. A sample jog-a-thon pledge sheet is shown in Figure 4-3.

The jog-a-thon is fun and almost everyone can participate, even if the student's idea of "jogging" is really "walking."

ACTIVITIES FOR JUNE

This is the time of year when students have the opportunity to summarize and evaluate what they have learned throughout the year. It is important that students have the chance to pull together for themselves some of the various ideas, skills, or feelings that might have been generated during the school year. This month's activities allow students to share this process with others.

Activity 1: People Bingo

GOAL: To allow students to summarize some of the events that have happened during the year.

Name	Amount Per Lap	Total Laps	Total

Figure 4–3

PROCEDURE: Form 4-8 is a Bingo chart. Make copies for every student in the class. As with other Bingo cards, each student must make a cross-match—either across, down, or diagonal. Allow students to move around the room to do this activity. If they find another student who can fulfill a certain block, then have that student sign his or her name in the block.

Activity 2: Class Sculpting

GOAL: To allow students to describe the interpersonal relations they have developed with others in the class.

PROCEDURE: Sculpting is a method whereby students actually plot their relationships with each other. They do this by placing themselves at the center and then grouping students around them in relation to how they feel about the others. Those students with whom they feel particularly close are placed closer to them than other students with whom they perhaps feel more distant. For example, Maryjo may feel that she has a better relationship with John than with any other in the room. In this case, she places John the closest to her.

This sculpting may be done in a number of forms. The easiest is to have the students do it on a piece of paper. Here, students use circles to represent the boys in the room, and triangles to represent the girls. If these symbols are made large enough, the students could also put a student's name or initials inside each shape, which would eliminate any confusion. Figure 4-4 is an example of how this could be done with four student names.

By this illustration, Maryjo is saying that she feels closer to John than anyone else in the class. Maryjo is also saying that she feels the girl, PQ, is more distant than John, but closer to her than the boy, MR. Furthermore, you could say the Maryjo feels that MR is closer to PQ than to J or MJ. Remember, this is Maryjo's feelings about the situation. The other students involved may draw different conclusions.

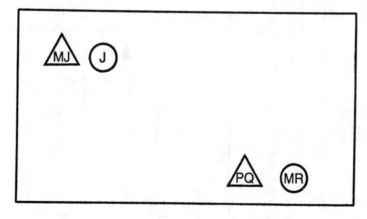

Figure 4–4

STUDENT BINGO

Find a person, and obtain the signature of one who . . .

Has helped me	Likes school	Has had a birthday in class
Has improved	Feels nervous in front of a group	Has five cents on him or her	Has been in the school two years	Is an old friend
Is coming back next year	Likes to cook	Is a new friend	Has won an award this year
Can spell well	Is a leader	Is a follower	Works well

Form 4-8

Another way to do class sculpting is to have the students actually place each other on the floor of the classroom in terms of closeness and distance. This can be fun, because it is live and involves actual movement of bodies. A third form of this activity is to have the students draw or use objects to describe others in the class, and then to use these drawings or objects to indicate closeness or distance.

Some teachers may feel that the class is not ready to reveal such delicate feelings about each other. In this case, just have the students complete the activity for their eyes only. Doing the activity is a learning experience in itself.

Activity 3: Class Evaluation

GOAL: To help students review the course for the year, and to help them summarize their feelings about what they learned.

PROCEDURE: You will need to review for yourself the entire course for the year. Notes that you took on each activity may be helpful in remembering the particulars. As you begin this activity, review the course with the students. You may want to mention some of the materials covered, some of the highlights, and some of the more enriching activities. Ask the students to describe some of the activities that they particularly liked.

At this point, distribute a copy of the evaluation sheet (see Form 4-9), and ask the students to complete it. Once the form is completed, students may want to share this with the entire class. You can then use this material to plan for next year's course.

Activity 4: Final Picnic

GOAL: To have the students plan and execute one final activity for the year; to have the students share each others' friendships; and to have a good time.

PROCEDURE: This picnic could be organized in a similar manner as the one completed in the fall. You will note major differences in how students get along during this picnic than the one held earlier. There should be more cooperation and sharing among the students.

CHAPTER 4 REFERENCES

Canfield, J., and H. C. Wells. *100 Ways To Enhance Self Concept in the Classroom.* Englewood Cliffs, NJ: Prentice Hall, 1976.

Demille, Richard. *Put Your Mother on the Ceiling; Children's Imagination Games.* New York: Viking Press, 1973.

Herzfeld, Gerald, and Robin Powell. *Coping for Kids: A Complete Stress Control Program for Students Ages 8-18.* West Nyack, NY: The Center for Applied Research in Education, 1986.

COURSE EVALUATION SHEET

1. What activity did you like the most, and why?

   _____

   _____

   _____

2. What activity did you enjoy the least, and why?

   _____

   _____

   _____

3. What did you learn about yourself this year?

   _____

   _____

   _____

4. What did you learn about others this year?

   _____

   _____

   _____

5. On a scale of 1 (having none) to 5 (having a lot), how would you describe this class?

Funny	1	2	3	4	5
Boring	1	2	3	4	5
Smart	1	2	3	4	5
Friendly	1	2	3	4	5
Angry	1	2	3	4	5
Supportive	1	2	3	4	5
Involved	1	2	3	4	5
_____	1	2	3	4	5
_____	1	2	3	4	5

Simon, S., L. Howe, and H. Kirschenbaum. *Values Clarification*. New York: Hart Publishers, 1972.

Thayer, Louis (ed.). *50 Strategies for Experiential Learning*. San Diego: University Associates, 1976.

chapter 5

DEALING WITH SPECIAL PROBLEMS

The four strategies discussed in this chapter were chosen because of their particular significance to the educational environment. Each in its own manner presents special problems to the classroom teacher in terms of providing a healthy, positive environment conducive to maximum learning. Special education teachers, in particular, are affected by these problems, because they have such a close personal relationship with all of the children assigned to their care. The special education teacher becomes the child's first line of rescue when he or she is seeking help from the burdens of society, of school, or of his or her own emotions. The techniques discussed in this chapter are geared for the special education teacher to apply directly to the particular situations these four problems may or may not cause in his or her classroom.

HOW TO COPE WITH AN ACUTE STUDENT EMOTIONAL CRISIS

As a special education teacher, you are more than likely to find yourself in a position of needing to respond to a student's emotional crisis. A child will often turn to a teacher that they know and trust for help during a crisis. This is even more true if his or her traditional support structure of the family is being attacked by the crisis. By crisis, we mean a problem or situation that overwhelms the person and his or her usual manner of solving problems. The reason for the person feeling overwhelmed may be the timing of the situation, the fact that the person was not prepared, or the fact that the traditional support resources upon which the person relied were not available.

When a student brings a crisis to your attention, you need to be prepared to handle it. It is not our task here to provide you with therapeutic techniques to help the child deal with the crisis on a long-term basis; that would be the role of the mental health team in the community. Our task is to give you some background knowledge of the dynamics of an emotional crisis, how a normal coping mechanism can turn abnormal, and how to apply psychological first aid to help the student, until a support and recovery team can be put in place to help the child deal with the crisis. This section is worth keeping handy, so that it is readily available for possible future use. When a student does make you aware of an emotional crisis, a quick re-reading of its contents will enable you to respond effectively to the crisis.

Four Ways to Cope with a Crisis

An emotional crisis can happen to anyone at any time. It is important to realize that a crisis is a normal part of living. Everyone experiences crises. Over the long term, a crisis may sometimes precipitate a positive learning experience, a personal growth experience, or even a creative opportunity in the individual. All of this may be comforting. Usually, however, when someone is in the midst of a crisis, it is difficult for that person to see beyond the immediate. The impact of a crisis can be so stunning that the individual is left helpless about how to deal with the change. Depending on their age, children will react differently. What may appear as indifference or apparent lack of acknowledgement on the part of a child may be a mask that covers a swirl of conflicting hurting emotions.

There are many models that describe how individuals handle crises. Some models approach crisis reaction as part of normal development; others view all reactions as pathological responses. All have incorporated steps or stages of crisis development. The most appropriate model seems to be one that incorporates a continuum of responses from normal to the pathological. As an individual moves through the stages of a crisis, his or her responses usually move along this continuum, ranging—at times—from the normal to the pathological. What concerns the teacher is the need for the child's response to return to the normal. The role of the teacher is to help monitor this response pattern and, when needed, to help the child respond with normal crisis reactions rather than pathological ones. Figure 5-1 shows a response pattern for crisis that is based on a continuum development model.

Techniques for Helping a Child Deal with a Crisis

The following techniques will help you deal with a child's crisis. Some of these techniques are adaptations from *The Crisis Intervention Handbook* by Brent Q. Hagen and Brenda Peterson (Englewood Cliffs, NJ: Prentice Hall, 1982).

STAGE 1:

Shock ——————————————— Immobilization

The sudden impact of the crisis produces feelings of anger, hopelessness, depression, fear, and panic. These feelings are conflicting and confusing. Sometimes, these feelings are not recognized. At the shock level, feelings are present, and there may be some awareness and recognition.

At the immobile level, the feelings overwhelm the individual to the point where all other functions are hampered or even stopped. There rarely is any recognition of one's feelings at this level.

STAGE 2:

Denial ——————————————— Delusion

After the sudden impact comes a period in which the feelings that were once very painful are put on hold. At this denial level, the child refuses to acknowledge any feelings about the event, and perhaps even the event itself.

At the delusion level, the child believes that things are, in fact, the same as they used to be before the crisis. The mind practically shuts down totally at this stage, having exhausted itself dealing with so many conflictual feelings at the first stage.

Figure 5–1

STAGE 3:

Acceptance ——————————————— Disorganization

With time, the body and mind return to a normal state. The child realizes that the crisis did occur and that there are consequences because of it. Something or someone has changed. At the acceptance level, the child starts to remember the details of the crisis. Memories and quick snapshot pictures intrude into the conscious, often while the child is working on something and busy. Perhaps, even some of the feelings will return for a moment or two. With little effort, the child is able to push these thoughts away; and there is little interruption in the task in which he or she is engaged. Next, a child starts to talk about the crisis. As the child begins to trust in his or her own recovery, he or she begins to trust others with some thoughts and feelings.

At the disorganization level, the child needs to work harder to keep the memory of the event away from his or her consciousness. Some older children will resort to chemical (drugs and/or alcohol) to help preserve the illusion that everything is all right. Depression follows, and, in some cases, suicide is attempted as the ultimate solution to keep the memory of the event away. In younger children, a pattern of hyperactivity is seen in school.

STAGE 4:

Reorganization ——————————————— Collapse

At this stage, the child is ready to get on with his or her life, having made adjustments for the consequences of the crisis. At the reorganizational level, the crisis is not forgotten, but the emotional language accompanying it has diminished. The anniversary of the event may still cause grief at the remembrance, but at this stage the child has learned mechanisms to cope with whatever hurt may return.

At the collapse level, there has been little successful attempt to handle the crisis. As a result, memories continue to persist and continue to disrupt the child's life. The wear and tear has its effects on the child's mind and body. Psychosomatic illnesses develop; study and concentration are difficult to maintain; regression of the maturity level appears; and, in general, the child begins to experience lifelong adjustment problems.

Figure 5—1 (continued)

1. REMEMBER YOUR GOAL.   The goal in any assistance is to monitor and help the progress a child will make as he or she moves through the four stages of the crisis. This progress may be rapid or may take years, depending on the situation, the particular crisis, and the personality of the child. It is important that you do not deprive a child of any one of these four *normal* stages. Remember that they are normal stages of reaction, and that each stage, in its own way, helps the child move toward discovering new methods of organizing and coping with life after the event.

If, however, you observe that the child is not following the normal stages of development but is continually having pathological responses to the crisis, you need to intervene. In almost all cases, you will need to seek professional medical and psychological help for the child. If the child shows signs of normal coping, but at times presents behavior that could be considered pathological, it is wise to offer support and assistance to help the child progress normally. Extra vigilance will be needed to assure a healthy reactive healing.

2. ACT QUICKLY.   If it is needed, provide medical help immediately. During the first stage, the child may be so overcome with feelings that he or she will have to be led to a quiet and protective place. Here, someone should remain with the child at all times. If you do not know the child, ask who he or she would like to see. What teacher or friend in the building does the child relate to? Inform the child that his or her parents have been called, or that the school is trying to locate them. Reassure the child that the parents will arrive at the school soon. Tell the child that he or she is safe now, and that the event is over, or that it cannot influence him or her now. This last statement may need to be said many times in many different ways. If the child is psychologically upset and is crying or shaking, hug him or her. If the child is older, hold his or her hand or grasp his or her shoulder. Make the child feel through nonverbal means that you are there. Encourage the child to talk even if only with gestures. Be relaxed during the silent periods.

3. ASSESS THE SITUATION.   You need to make some judgments about how seriously the child has been affected by the crisis. Obviously, medical needs are a priority, but as soon as these needs are stabilized, you will need to respond to emotional needs. Ask open-ended questions about the event even if you know the answer. Try to get the child to verbalize the event. Ask questions, such as, "What happened just now?"; "What were you doing?"; "How did you learn about it?"; "How come you are involved?" If a child will not respond to you and you are someone he or she knows, then you have a clue that perhaps this child is responding to the first stage by a pathological immobile response.

4. DO SOMETHING QUICKLY.   If you observe the beginnings of immobilization, do something with the child. Have the child make a phone call, walk around the school with you, go to the bathroom, eat or drink something, or watch TV while he or she waits. Start talking to the child even if there is no verbal

response. Talk about anything but the crisis. Try to start a conversation with the child. Ask the child to begin by nodding his or her head.

5. LISTEN ACTIVELY.   Listening is a skill that needs to be learned. You need to learn to listen for content and for feelings. A child needs to know that you will understand, care for, and support him or her through the crisis. Listed below are a few guidelines to improve your active listening skills.

Listen for Content. Repeat to the child what he or she has just said to you. You can do this by using the same words the child uses or, as illustrated below in our example with Eddie, by paraphrasing the content. You can do this a few times at the beginning of the dialogue to demonstrate that you are truly trying to understand the child.

> BILLY: And my father hit my mother and...
> TEACHER: Your father hit your mother.

or, you may say:

> EDDIE: When the bus turned over, I screamed. I ran over others . . . a mess . . . I was scared, but I ran.
> TEACHER: The bus turned over and you ran, even though you were scared.

More than likely, the child will respond to this listening for content by saying, "Yes," "That's right," or give you some other form of acknowledgement that your response was correct. If the child feels that what you said was wrong, he or she will tell you. Regardless, you are demonstrating a desire to understand.

Listen for Feelings. Here you need to listen for "feeling" words a child may be using. You need to repeat these to the child to show that you do understand and also to help the child become aware of the feelings that he or she is expressing. If the child does not use "feeling" words, as in our case with Wendy, you will need to make a guess about how the child is feeling. If you guess wrong, the child will correct you.

> SUE: I get so frustrated with him.
> TEACHER: You are frustrated.

Or

> WENDY: Walking there, and then working all day, and not getting anything done with Ben.
> TEACHER: You seem frustrated.

6. SET A LIMITED GOAL.   Work to do something with the child right after the immediate part of the crisis is over. These activities may include visiting someone, finding and reading a book on the crisis, writing a letter, or doing something else that is concrete. If the child is in Stage Two, at which stage, denial is operative, remain supportive. Do not confront the denial, but gently remind the child that the two of you need to set a goal. Focusing on the goal will make the crisis real enough for the child and will help move him or her toward the acceptance stage. Often, elementary-school-aged children will talk about their crisis in some detail, but they will appear void of any emotion related to it. This is also a form of denial, and their responses should be handled gently.

7. ASSESS A PERSON'S SUPPORT SYSTEM.   Depending on the crisis, you will need to mobilize a school/community recovery and support team for the child. If you are the teacher the child trusts, become an active part of this team. You are in a perfect position to coordinate the various services if the parent or guardian is not adequate for the task. Also, if you are involved, the child will feel more comfortable in talking to you about the crisis events.

8. PLAN FOR THE FUTURE.   Help lead the child from the acceptance to the reorganization stage by helping him or her make future plans. You can help the child find alternative ways to accomplish similar goals. You will need to confront unrealistic plans. For example, Regina planned to visit her father in prison for his birthday. Unfortunately, no minors were allowed in the prison. The teacher, in this case, helped Regina find alternative ways to share her birthday. Through this planning process, a teacher can show support and keep communications open.

Dealing with a School-wide Crisis

There are occasions when the entire school population experiences a crisis. A recent example was the space shuttle Challenger blowing up at liftoff while all children at certain schools were watching the event on closed circuit TV. The reactions of children to such an event will vary from individual to individual. Some students will cry; some will sit in shock; and others will go about their business as if nothing has happened. How does a classroom teacher handle such an uncontrolled event? Here are a few suggestions:

1. Suspend instruction for a while. Students will be too upset to learn; moreover, even a tragic event like the Challenger can be a learning experience for the children.
2. Expose the children to information. Either turn on the TV, or have someone in authority come to the room to provide a report of events. The national news coverage of the Challenger provided full information about what happened.

3. Talk about the event. Ask students what they know, what they saw, and what they heard. Ask for opinions about what happened. If the TV is on, ask students to comment on what they are seeing. At times, turn the set off, and explain to the children what has happened, or what is happening.

4. Be calm, relaxed and self-confident. Students should be made to feel that they and you will be able to handle the discussion of the crisis. The students need to look at you as one who can handle emotion. You will be their model.

5. Plan something that will capture the students' feelings, and channel their energies into something constructive. On the day of the Challenger accident, students in one school signed and sent a six-foot by two-foot long sympathy card to the students of the high school where the teacher-in-space had taught. This card was a symbol of the students' grief, and also a symbol of hope and an expression of solidarity with other students.

Remember that a student with an emotional crisis needs help. The help that you as a teacher can provide can be the psychological first aid the child may need to survive the first few hours or days of the crisis. You are in a perfect position to provide support, care, and hope. All three are the basic ingredients of recovery. Your knowledge of the four stages of recovery and the continuum model of responses will provide a framework to assess, monitor, and assist a student to recover to the normal stage. Effecting change over the duration of the crisis is a task for an outside support and recovery team. However, by using some of the suggestions in this section, you will be in a position to move quickly to heal the child's emotional wounds. [Note: An excellent resource that treats this topic is *The Compassionate School: A Practical Guide to Educating Abused and Traumatized Children*, by Gertrude Morrow (Englewood Cliffs, NJ: Prentice-Hall, 1987).]

A PREVENTIVE APPROACH TO STUDENT SUICIDE

For those teachers working with teens, it comes as no surprise to hear that suicide is the second leading cause of death among this age group. While the rate of suicide among other age groups has declined since 1968, it has increased by 72 percent for the adolescent age group. More alarming is the reported incidents of attempted suicide to actual suicidal deaths. According to David Curran in *Adolescent Suicidal Behavior* (New York: Hemisphere Publishing Corporation, 1987, 14-15), this figure ranges between 200 and 312 to 1.

Prevention of suicide can begin in the schools. In fact, the school can play a pivotal role in addressing the major problems of depression, the leading psychological cause of suicide. The focus of this section is to provide the classroom teacher with a number of classroom activities that can help students deal with their feelings about death and suicide. This section will not be helpful to a teacher with a child who has expressed the intent to commit suicide. In this case, the teacher should have referred the matter to the school's mental health team. Just a word of caution—all expressions of potential self-inflicted death should be taken seriously. Help should be provided immediately, and the adult should remain with the child until the appropriate resource person arrives to deal with the situation.

This section is geared for the child 10 and older. While there is growing evidence that suicide is present in younger children, there is a great need to address the psychological needs of children in the pre-adolescent and adolescent age range. It is at this age that children are capable of understanding what death is about, and it is also at this age that suicide is talked about and, perhaps, even contemplated.

Figure 5-2 reproduces a letter found on a 12-year-old girl who had gone into the girl's bathroom and swallowed a large dosage of aspirins. While the child was saved, this letter presents a vivid account of the confused and painful feelings that swirled inside her at the time of her attempted suicide. The spelling and punctuation are hers.

The program outlined below can be run with 10 to 13 students. It is best that the group have members of both sexes. This presentation is only suggested. As a teacher, you will need to adapt it to your individual needs.

Session 1

Present the goals of this course. For example, you might say that, twice a week for the next three weeks, you will be presenting some information about adolescent suicide. Tell the children you are doing this to help them, because you are alarmed at the danger and the level this increasing trend has reached. You might give them some ideas or on overview of what you will be teaching for the next few weeks. Topics should include facts and myths about suicide, warning signs, how you can

---

Toni,
What's up? have girl how are you doing. me I'am doing just. the only reason I write you last night it was just because I very up set and you know why. and the real reason is because I knew he's going to say no and that's not what I need and I know you can really tell that I like him is because I never tell a boy I like him before I can tell he have feelings for me and that's the real reason why I'am scared.

Well have to go have no more to say well see you maybe
I hope your friend

                                    Rose

Figure 5–2

help a friend, and, possibly, referral sources. Mention that there will be time to discuss any recent suicides in the community.

Distribute Forms 5-1 and 5-2. Hold a general discussion about each item on these information sheets as you read through the sheets as a group.

Session 2

"Preventing Teen Suicide: You Can Help" is an excellent filmstrip on suicide that can be the source of numerous discussions. (The filmstrip is available from: Sunburst Communications, 101 Castleton Avenue, Pleasantville, NY 10570.)

Session 3

Ask the children to take one character in the film and to list separately what each character knew and did about the situation. The characters are the following:

- English teacher
- Girl
- Brother
- Friend
- Boyfriend

The next step is to assign an emotion to each character. Some emotion words you might ask the class to assign are these:

depressed	outraged	good
lost	out-of-it	uptight
unsure	regretful	hurt
moody	cheerful	left out
happy	thrilled	excited
pleased	trapped	bad

Session 4

This session will be devoted to how to identify pressures in our life, and how to develop positive means of dealing with them.

Ask students to discuss sources of pressure. Some examples:

- Peer pressure
- School pressure
- Teacher pressure
- Parent pressure
- Community pressure

FACTS AND FABLES ABOUT SUICIDE*

Fable: People who talk about suicide don't commit suicide.
Fact: Of any ten persons who kill themselves, eight have given definite warnings of their suicidal intentions.

Fable: Suicide happens without warning.
Fact: Studies reveal the suicidal person gives many clues and warnings regarding his or her suicidal intentions.

Fable: Suicidal people are fully intent on dying.
Fact: Most suicidal people are undecided about living or dying, and they "gamble with death," leaving it to others to save them. Almost no one commits suicide without letting others know how he or she is feeling.

Fable: Once a person is suicidal, he or she is suicidal forever.
Fact: Individuals who wish to kill themselves are suicidal only for a limited period of time.

Fable: Improvement following a suicidal crisis means that the suicidal risk is over.
Fact: Most suicides occur within roughly three months following the beginning of "improvement," when the individual has the energy to put his or her morbid thoughts and feelings into effect.

Fable: Suicide strikes more often among the rich—or, conversely, it occurs almost exclusively among the poor.
Fact: Suicide is neither a rich man's disease nor the poor man's curse. Suicide is very "democratic," and it is represented proportionately among all levels of society.

Fable: Suicide is inherited or "runs in families."
Fact: Suicide does not run in families. It is an individual pattern.

Fable: All suicidal individuals are mentally ill, and suicide is always the act of a psychotic person.
Fact: Studies of genuine suicide notes indicate that although the suicidal person is extremely unhappy, he or she is not necessarily mentally ill.

© 1988 by The Center for Applied Research in Education

Form 5-1

*From *Some Facts About Suicide,* Public Health Publication No. 852, U.S. Government Printing Office, 1961.

DEPRESSION AND SUICIDE

Warning Signals

- Deep depression
- Withdrawal from family and friends
- Drop in grades
- Drop in activities such as hobbies, sports
- Major loss of a steady boyfriend/girlfriend
- Eating and/or sleeping habits change
- Outbursts of unusual or reckless behavior
- Giving away treasured possessions
- Preoccupation with the subject of death
- Talk of suicide or worthlessness
- Personal neglect

Facts and Figures

1. Approximately 5,000 young people between the ages of 10 and 19 kill themselves each year.

2. Suicide is the second leading cause of death among young people. (The first is accidents.)

3. Twice as many teenagers commit suicide today as did ten years ago.

4. 250,000 teenagers will attempt suicide this year.

5. Girls attempt suicide on a ratio of eight times for every time a boy does. However, boys actually do kill themselves on a ratio of three times for every time a girl does. The reason for the reverse in figures is that boys generally choose more violent means of killing themselves and therefore are more successful the first time.

Form 5-2

Ask students to decide which pressure in their lives is the hardest to deal with. A song by Billy Joel, "Pressure," could be played and discussed.

Have the students complete Form 5-3. Have them choose an emotion, such as sad, angry, lonely, or frustrated, to fill in the blanks.

Ask the students to discuss their worksheets. Often, comments from one student will help another. Some students may not want to share their comments, and these feelings are acceptable and should be honored.

To conclude the session, the teacher might discuss other ways of handling pressure. The session should end on an upbeat note and leave students with the hope and belief that stress is a common characteristic of life, that it generates emotions, and, most important, that it can be dealt with.

Session 5

This session will help students discover why some children view suicide as the only method available to deal with pressure.

If you have the opportunity to clip newspaper articles about a recent suicide in your community, you could share these with the students. If you have no articles, you could share the letter of Rose that is reproduced above. Discuss the meaning of depression with the students. In particular, point out that children choose suicide, because the pressure and strain become so great that they cannot bear these feelings any longer. They become emotionally exhausted; and, as fatigue sets in, they just give up.

Ask the students to name places where they could go to get help if they felt emotionally wiped out and depressed. List the places, and even the individuals, the students mention. Always add the number of the local suicide hot-line phone to the end of the list.

Next, have the students brainstorm ideas they use to overcome depression and sadness. Some of the ideas that will be presented will be very sound, and others will seem zany, but may work. List all the ideas. Encourage students to try one of them the next time they are feeling depressed.

The final part of this session is to discuss with students the need to let people in authority know if one of their friends is talking about suicide. Remind the students that a person who talks to them about committing suicide is asking for help. The job of the friend is to get help, not to keep the wish a secret. A great theme to push is, "Keep a secret, lose a friend." This theme will remind students to take suicide threats seriously.

Session 6

This session, which should be held about one month after the first series of sessions, is essentially a follow-up session. Bring up the topic of adolescent suicide again, and review some of the major points made in the last sessions. Ask the students if they have tried any new stress reduction techniques during the past month that have worked successfully. Discuss and share with students the need to

FEELINGS WORKSHEET

Situations that make me _____ :

a. _____

_____

_____

b. _____

_____

_____

c. _____

_____

_____

How I deal with being _____ :

a. _____

_____

_____

b. _____

_____

_____

c. _____

_____

_____

Form 5-3

find a personal stress reduction behavior. If time permits, conduct the activity, "Share-a-Concern." (Refer to Chapter 4 March activities.)

HOW TO SOLVE STUDY PROBLEMS

All students have a need to learn how to study more efficiently. Preparing to study, test-taking, notetaking, doing a research paper, and even methods to read a textbook or newspaper are skills that can be taught and practiced. By reviewing these skills periodically, a teacher can drill students on the necessary skills to survive in classrooms. This section will demonstrate a method of teaching study skills. If students in your classroom have problems in one of the five study-skill areas mentioned above, you may wish to take some time to teach these skills.

Effective Study

The goal of this section is to teach students how to work faster and get more done. It will enable students to organize their study habits so that they will know when, where, and how to study. This section is particularly useful to students who need to study at home or in the library, where the structure and management aids of the classroom are not available. Whether the student is doing grade-level work or is at a self-caring level of functioning, these skills will be helpful.

TIME.   The first step is to determine the optimal time and location for study. The time should be fairly consistent each day; it should be "booked" for study. For some students, it may be lunch time, a study hall, before school, after school, or after dinner. The chart in Form 5-4 divides the school day into specific time slots. By completing it, the student will determine the best study time. Have the student put an X in the time he or she is free during the day. By free, we mean the student has no obligations, such as being in class, walking the dog, or doing the paper route. In the second box, the student should indicate with another X whether or not this is a good time to study. Although a student may have lunch free, the noise and lack of privacy may prevent him or her from finding good conditions to study. The question the student needs to ask is whether the time indicated as free is a time when he or she is not tired, not distracted and can find some privacy. The final box is a place where the student can indicate where he or she will or could be to find the best study conditions. The place also needs to be free of distractions and have a table and chair, proper lighting, and suitable materials needed for study. Upon completion of this time chart, the student will be in a position to determine the best time of day to study.

ASSIGNMENT.   Make sure the student understands the study assignment. At the end of the school day, write the homework on the board, and allow students enough time to copy it. Write the homework assignment in the same form each day, so the students are not confused in writing it down. Form 5-5 will help you design your own form—or you may want to use the form as is. This layout could be

STUDY TIME CHART

Time	Possible Free Time	Good Study Time	Place
7:00 A.M.–10:00 A.M.			
10:00 A.M.– 2:00 P.M.			
2:00 P.M.– 4:00 P.M.			
4:00 P.M.– 6:00 P.M.			
6:00 P.M.–10:00 P.M.			

Form 5-4

ASSIGNMENT FORM

Date:_____

Goal:_____

Task: Book:_____ Pages:_____

_____

_____

_____

_____

Comments:_____

_____

_____

Check when completed:_____

Form 5-5

inserted in the student's notebook for easy reference. In addition to writing out the assignments, explain it. A section in the assignment is left for comments you may wish to make. As for any other new task in September, you will need to check and retrain students on how to record the assignment. However, after a few repetitions, the students will remember and be able to use the form with ease. The last helpful hint in this section is to provide the students with at least one backup telephone number of a classmate. In case the assignment is lost or forgotten, the student can call this backup for the assignment. Make sure to tell students that the backup phone number should not only be written in their assignment notebooks.

ARRANGEMENT.   All assignments are not equal in difficulty or importance. Both of these characteristics can vary, according to the child. A student may need help determining in what order to study the material. Perhaps, the harder task should be done first, and the easier task done later when fatigue may set in. Perhaps, different times of the day are better for the completion of the harder tasks. If an assignment is long-term, the student will need to be taught how to pace the work so that he or she does not end up making an impossible attempt to complete the entire task the night before it is due.

To complete Form 5-6, the student should list the assignments in the left-hand column and then rank the assignments as to order of difficulty. For example, learning five spelling words overnight might be considered harder than reading two pages of a magazine. In the extreme right-hand column, the student can indicate at what time of the day this assignment will be completed. Perhaps, the students will decide to study the spelling words at home after dinner and to do the reading assignment that can be done quickly in the school's study hall. For long-term assignments, this schedule could be converted into a more lengthy time schedule.

MATERIALS.   The place where a student studies should have the necessary equipment for him or her to complete the assignment. Certainly, pens, pencils, paper, ruler, dictionary, and an eraser are needed, and these should be ready for use. A student can waste a great deal of time each night looking for a sharpened pencil. Care should also be taken to make sure a table, or desk, and a chair are present for the student's use. A quick call to the parents at the beginning of each school year will help ensure that the necessary equipment is in place for the student. It is also a good idea to remind the student around midyear about the need to reequip his or her study area.

Effective Notetaking

Notetaking is part listening, part observing, and part organization. A student who can take notes that are readable, contain relevant comments, and are organized for quick review is a student who will comprehend more and be able to relate this information to other pieces of information learned elsewhere. To begin with, every student should have a notebook available. A three-ring binder is handy, because it

ARRANGEMENT SCHEDULE

Assignment	Difficulty	When to Be Done

Form 5-6

puts all the material together in one place. Notes themselves can be written words, drawn pictures, or even pictures cut from magazines.

In teaching notetaking, show the student a short piece of film. The subject matter of the film need only be age-appropriate and interesting. After 15 minutes, stop the film, and ask the students to record one main idea from the film. Then, when everyone has recorded one idea, ask the students to record two things that they saw in the film which describe this idea. For example,

Main Idea:	Adventure film
Two Things That Happened:	There was a storm.
	There was a wild animal.

Now, you need to teach students how to label these two items. The main idea is numerically labeled, beginning with a "1." The subtopic ideas are labeled "A" through "Z." So, an example looks like this:

1. Adventure film
   A. Storm
   B. Wild animal

You now have taught your students how to outline subject matter. This outline should go into the notebooks. Make sure each student labels the top of the page in the notebook with a title of the course and what is being studied. The date should also be included. Enough space should be left between these outlines for the student or the teacher to add comments.

Notes a student takes during a class should be assigned for homework to review. Some students even rewrite their notes to reorganize their own observations about the lesson. Notes can be a handy record of each lesson and, if reviewed frequently, serve as a very helpful tool for total lesson comprehension. Form 5-7 is an exercise your students can use to practice notetaking skills.

Effective Test-Taking

Students of today take many tests. Some tests are national- or state-standardized, and others are the traditional classroom tests of teachers. The forms used on these various tests also differ. Essay, multiple-choice, fill-in-the-blank, matching, and true and false are but a few of the varied forms. Understanding how to study for a test and how to attack the questions on a test are skills every student needs to know. With such knowledge, students are bound to improve their test scores.

PREPARATION.   Have the student write in his or her assignment book the subject of the test, and when it will be given. If you are accustomed to announcing page numbers in a text or specific issues, make sure the students write this information down. You might even tell them the form of the test. This prepares students and also helps define the type of study that will be conducted.

For the actual study procedure, make sure the students review their notebooks and are able to list the main ideas that have been covered in the past lessons.

PRACTICE IN OUTLINING

Listed on the left are four main ideas. Listed on the right are a number of subtopics or observations about the main ideas. Write the main ideas in the format provided, and list the correct subtopics.

Social Studies	Earthquakes
Math	Spelling
English	1492
Science	Addition
	George Washington
	Vocabulary
	Subtraction
	Electricity

1. _____

   A. _____

   B. _____

2. _____

   A. _____

   B. _____

3. _____

   A. _____

   B. _____

4. _____

   A. _____

   B. _____

Ask the students to write down these main ideas, and then to write a comment about each one. Have the students circle the most important main ideas. If students seem confused about any of the main ideas, ask them to check with a friend, reread the text, or ask for help. If there is time, the student can make up questions and attempt to answer them. For some students, verbally rehearsing the important issues is helpful. For others, reviewing a series of photos or magazine cutouts helps pull the related material together.

TAKING THE TEST.   Students should always read the test directions. Make sure they are doing what they should be doing. Have them skim through the entire test first. Make sure they plan on doing each test section within a certain amount of time. Remind them to budget time carefully. If they do not know an answer, have them circle the question and come back to it. Remind them not to spend extra time solving one hard question. Unless otherwise directed, they should answer *all* questions, even if they have to guess.

The strategies involved in solving each of the different types of questions are listed here. They are written in a form that you can read to the students:

- *Essay:* As you read the question, underline important words, such as "describe," "compare," and "comment on." These words tell you what to do. Now brainstorm as many ideas as you can think of about the topic. Make a mental picture of it. Write a main idea based on one of your ideas, and list two subtopics. Use the notetaking form described earlier. You now have an outline. Make a sentence or two of the main idea. Be sure to include one of the key words you have already underlined. For example, you might say, "An example of good ice cream is Sal and Suzy's double vanilla." Use the subtopic ideas to explain the main idea further. Write one sentence to summarize your thoughts. Reread the essay for spelling and grammar.

- *Multiple Choice:* Read the question while covering the answers. Try to answer the question without looking at the answers. Then, look at the answers to see if there is a match between one of the choices and yours. Cross out those answers you know are not true. Try to find one reason why one of the remaining answers could be right. Questions that confuse you should be circled and skipped. If time permits, go back to those questions.

- *Matching Questions:* Read the directions. Look at one list, and then the other. Cross out those you know. Guess answers for the remaining unknown matches.

- *True and False:* You have a 50-50 chance of getting this type of question right. Answer those you know first. Then decide on the others by looking for clue words to trick you. Statements beginning with "all," "never," or "only" can be misleading. The statements must be correct 100 percent of the time; make sure the statements you pick are correct 100 percent of the time.

As a teacher, you can make up sample types of tests using the different forms. Ask the students to practice just taking tests. Relieve the pressure by not grading the work. Rather, have the students experiment taking tests.

Effective Reading

Reading a textbook, magazine, or study workbook can be a laborious process for many students. Many students have poor reading vocabulary, which adds to the problem of comprehension. How does a student retain the important facts from this material? Following a few guidelines, it is possible to teach students to retain more from their reading.

The first step is to tell the students that they never, never should begin reading a book by starting with page 1. Long before they begin to read, they should ask themselves a few questions and follow some necessary procedures:

1. Glance through the book looking at pictures and diagrams.
2. Glance at the Table of Contents. How does the author break down or divide his topic of study?
3. Review each chapter to determine the organization of the chapter material. How many subsections does each chapter contain? How are colored sections used?
4. Read the introduction and the final summary (if it exists). Does the author say the same thing in both parts of the book? Does the summary section answer or address the needs and problems mentioned in the introduction?
5. Read the first and last paragraph in every chapter. Are the two paragraphs related in any manner? If they do mention common things, what can you learn about the chapter?
6. Choose a chapter (usually the first), and read the first sentence of each paragraph. What have you learned so far?
7. Determine what this book, magazine, or study workbook is going to teach you. What questions will be answered by reading this chapter?

Now you are ready to read the book or magazine from word to word. Enjoy the literary experience, since you have already done your organizational work in understanding how the text is presented and what questions it will answer for you. At the end of each chapter, sum up what you have read in a few words. Use the outline technique demonstrated earlier to choose the main idea and some subtopics of the chapter.

Effective Research

It is not uncommon for special-education students to have research topics required of them. While this is more likely for secondary-level, learning-disabled students in mainstream classes, other students in special education are sometimes given research assignments. In fact, it is an excellent idea for all students, regardless of their learning background, to be given the experience of researching a topic. The learning process itself for completion of a research task involves mastery of skills related to organization, searching, observing, reading, notetaking, and writing. All children should have these skills, regardless of their background. Form 5-8 will help students in the research process.

HOW TO TEACH CONFLICT RESOLUTION SKILLS

This section will be particularly helpful to you if you are teaching children who have problems relating to people with whom they are in conflict. These people could be parents, adults in the school building, other children, or even yourself. The quetion that needs to be explored is how do children deal with conflictual relations. Very often, the social skills associated with resolving conflicts are not developed in children. The result of such lack of skill development can spell disaster for many children.

If you take a minute to reflect on how conflict resolution skills are developed, you can assume that most children learn these vital skills through many forums: parent-modeling, viewing other adults deal with conflict, personal trial-and-error experiences, and training. For many children who lack these skills, there is an inadequacy of appropriate adult role-models in their lives. Personal trial-and-error experiences are unfulfilled, because there is a lack of feedback on what works and what does not. In addition, you have many special-education children who are developmentally immature, so they cannot grasp the essence of the social relation, let alone develop the skills necessary to take control of the situation. For many children who have lags in their social-skill development, training is an important component of their social education. In this section, the reader will find a social-skills training program for special-education children. The program is presented with a number of different levels of training that can be applied. The appropriate level depends on the maturity and needs of the student.

Overview

There are three primary methods through which children—also, adults for that matter—deal with a social conflict:

- Fight
- Flight
- Assertiveness

Let's look at each of these in order to gain an understanding of what works and what does not work.

THE RESEARCH PROCESS

Topic Selection

Pick a topic you are interested in finding out more about. If you are a bit unsure, ask your teacher to assign you a topic. Write your topic here.

_____

Initial Statement

Write a few sentences about your topic. You might say why you chose it, what you hope to learn, and what questions it will solve. List your sentences here.

_____

_____

_____

_____

Search

This is the fun part. Go to the school library and ask the librarian to help you find books, articles, filmstrips, magazines, and other resources that will tell you about the topic. There may also be a teacher in the building who could be a great source of information about this topic.

Outline

Once you put together a few ideas about your topic, prepare an outline. Using the format discussed in notetaking, prepare a few main ideas with subtopics to explain each idea. Write them here.

1._____

   A._____

   B._____

2._____

   A._____

   B._____

© 1988 by The Center for Applied Research in Education

Search Again

Take your outline back to the librarian and ask for help on either the main idea or one of the subtopics. Once again, read to gain more information about the topic. List all the sources of information that have helped you so far. These can be books, articles, and so on.

Revise Others

This time, make changes in your outline. Perhaps, you would like to delete or add a subtopic. Write a sentence or two about each main idea and subtopic. Record these here.

1._____

   A._____

   B._____

2._____

   A._____

   B._____

Write Rough Copy

Now is the time to put the sentences together in a paragraph. Add an introduction to this paragraph by using the initial statement you wrote earlier under "Initial Statement." Add a summary section by adding one sentence about how you felt doing the search and what you learned. The format should look like this:

Topic (from "Topic Selection"):_____

_____

Introduction (from "Initial Statement"):_____

_____

_____

_____

Form 5-8 (continued)

Paragraph (Main Idea #1 and subtopics):_____

_____

_____

_____

Paragraph (Main Idea #2 and subtopics):_____

_____

_____

_____

Summary: I learned that_____

_____

_____

I felt that_____

_____

_____

Sources (list the references from "Search Again"):_____

_____

_____

_____

_____

_____

Form 5-8 (continued)

FIGHT.   Robert is a thin, slightly impoverished looking ten-year-old boy who has been referred to the Committee on the Handicapped, because he is constantly fighting with his classmates. Robert is often teased by his classmates for things he says, the way he looks, and the way he dresses. Robert usually reacts to these taunts by physically attacking his opponent. In school, he is known to have "a short fuse." Ironically, despite his aggressiveness, Robert usually is the one who receives the most damage from the physical assaults.

While it is not our intention to psychoanalyze Robert, it is helpful to mention the dynamics behind his fight behavior. Most people who are aggressive act so because they have a great internal fear that they are not in control, or will lose control, of a situation. Based on this insecure need, they react in a very aggressive manner to present an image both to themselves and to others that they are, in fact, in control. While this representation is an illusion, it does become reality for the Roberts of our own schools.

For a special-education teacher to deal with Robert, he or she will need to deal with Robert's fear of losing control. Robert will need to learn to substitute new skills to replace his socially inappropriate "fight" control mechanism. If Robert does not make this substitution, he is doomed to a life of frustration, fear, physical harm, and perhaps the criminal courts.

FLIGHT.   Jerry is a secure person. Nothing bothers him, and he is seen by his teacher and special services team as a nice boy with no special problems. The fact that Jerry has a learning disability and requires support from the building's Resource Room does not point to a need in terms of relating to others, especially when relating to others over a conflictual issue. If observers asked Jerry's teachers about how Jerry deals with conflictual relations, more than likely they would say that Jerry has no instances of conflicts with others. In fact, they would report that Jerry is a nice boy and is well liked by one and all. And herein lies Jerry's problem: he has no conflicts, because he avoids conflicts with others. Jerry is secure, because he has a protective "flight" mechanism through which he protects and defends himself.

The dynamics in Jerry's case are quite simple. Unlike Robert who seeks control for fear of losing control, Jerry seeks no control. He is content in letting others—his friends, his teacher, and his parents—make the decisions about his life. He lets others assume what should be his responsibility. As a result, he is happy when things are going well; when things are not going well, he sits back and avoids the conflict. He lets issues be resolved for him, and only then does he assume his duties. For example, Jerry's special-education class went on a field trip to the zoo. On the bus, two of Jerry's classmates ate his lunch. Jerry just watched them eat it; he did not protest or tell the teachers on the bus. While at the zoo, Jerry had nothing to eat at lunch time. No one noticed. At the end of the day, the teachers rated the trip a success; and even Jerry, despite his hungry stomach, said he had a great time.

The task of Jerry's special-education teacher is to teach him to be less "nice" and more assertive. Jerry needs to learn to substitute new assertive skills for his socially inappropriate "flight" control mechanism. If Jerry does not make this substitution, he is doomed to a life of frustration, irresponsibility, lack of respect from others, and a lack of control over his life.

ASSERTION.   John is a ten-year-old mentally handicapped child. He has a long history of not only learning problems but also social problems. John has been known to become involved in fights and also to avoid situations that are potentially conflictual. He has displayed both fight and flight behavior. Lately, however, John has learned a new skill and has learned to use this skill to deal with the one girl in his class who is constantly teasing him. Mary Jo has learned that she can confuse John easily. She will tell him to do something; when John attempts the task, she will tell him to do it in a completely different way. John, as a result, becomes confused and intimidated. He has been known to throw pens or to go hide in the closet when he feels this way. Mary Jo receives great satisfaction from this behavior, and she obtains social approval when the others in the class laugh at John's response.

The teacher has witnessed this situation many times and realizes that John reacts to Mary Jo as he does because he is confused. He does not know how to react appropriately to Mary Jo. The teacher decides to teach John one specific assertive response to Mary Jo's demands. The teacher chooses one response only and makes it specific to the case because of John's limited mental ability. He probably would have trouble applying a general assertive response to the details of Mary Jo's situation.

The response taught was simple and concise. When Mary Jo told John what to do, John responded by saying, "Thank you, but I will ask the teacher." When Mary Jo persisted, John repeated this response. He was taught to repeat it as many times as necessary until Mary Jo left him alone. Note that the teacher did not elaborate on this assertive response. She did not require John to look Mary Jo in the eye, to raise his voice, or even to tell her to leave him alone—all appropriate responses. For John, the task was simple, assumable, and, most important, result-oriented.

Teaching Assertive Skills

Teaching assertive skills to students who need to learn how to respond to conflictual social situations presents a more direct, effective manner of relating than the traditional fight or flight methods most students use. Using assertive skills demands something in return from students. First, it demands that students become involved in the situation certainly longer than a flight response, and probably longer than a fight one. It requires that the involvement be verbal, positive, face-saving, and result-oriented. All of these characteristics are absent in the fight or flight alternatives. Second, using assertive skills demands that students risk part of themselves once they become engaged. They will certainly be misunderstood at first, perhaps teased, and most assuredly reacted to in some manner or other. To the Jerry's of the world, the flight response will, at times, be very appealing. Third, using assertive skills will produce results. Something will happen. The result cannot be totally planned, and here is the risk. In our example of Mary Jo, John cannot control or even predict what Mary Jo's response will be. However, the final result will make John feel good, and it will relieve John of Mary Jo's persistent teasing. Ultimately, it will give John control over his social situation.

Methods of Assertiveness

There are different levels of assertiveness for which a student could be trained. However, there are five basic principles a teacher should be aware of in attempting to train anyone in how to use assertive skills:

1. Make the behavior specific. Whatever it is you are teaching the student to say or do, make sure it is simple, brief, and related to a real issue or problem.
2. Pick those situations for which a student can use assertive skills and win. There are situations which no amount of assertiveness—or flight or fight behavior for that matter—will change.
3. Be sure to be consistent. If you are going to use assertive behavior, use it every time the same situation arises. If a child is assertive one day and gets appropriate results but on the next day uses "flight" behavior, the consistency is lost, and so is the power of the assertive behavior. To an outsider, it might seem logical to provoke the student if there is a 50 percent chance the student will run away.
4. Make no judgments. When you are assertive, you really should not care about why someone does or says something to annoy you. Making inferences about motives, attitudes, or character is mind-reading behavior or psychological game-playing. Trying to infer why may satisfy curiosity, but it does not help in producing assertive behavior. It is best to teach the assertive skill and worry about why something is done later.
5. Always make the assertive skill to be taught a genuine skill the student can adopt. For example, asking a shy student to raise her voice and make eye contact with the class bully would most likely be so out of character for the student that this assertive skill would not work and probably would embarrass the student.

Levels of Assertive Behavior

There are three basic levels of assertive behavior:

-   Beginning assertive skills
-   Intermediate assertive skills
-   Advanced assertive skills

Let's take a closer look at each one.

BEGINNING ASSERTIVE SKILLS.   This is the initial entry level of assertive behavior. It employs clear and concise responses to social situations that may or may not be considered conflictual. These techniques are ideal for students of limited mental ability or for students who are extremely withdrawn.

1. *Saying No.* Using this procedure, a student responds very clearly by stating his or her opinion about something someone else has asked him or her to do.

> BILLY: Come on, Marty, let's cut this class.
> MARTY: No.

2. *Persistence.* Using this procedure, a student can ward off continuous verbal requests from another until the other gives up. Using our previous example:

> MARY JO: John, you are supposed to go to the bathroom now.
> JOHN: I do not have to go.
> MARY JO: But you must.
> JOHN: I do not have to go.
> MARY JO: But you always do as I say.
> JOHN: I do not have to go.
> MARY JO: Forget the teacher. She is not watching.
> JOHN: I do not have to go.
> MARY JO: Aw, I give up.

3. *Ask for Help.* This skill disarms the opponent in any verbal confrontation.

> EDDIE: If you were a better student, you would get A's.
> STEVIE: Perhaps you can help me get A's.

4. *Ignore It.* The chief thing to remember about this skill is to ignore the behavior of the other, not to ignore the person.

> BERT: Ernie, you always do dumb things in gym class.
> ERNIE: Hey, Bert, let's go over to the other side of the gym.

5. *Be Direct.* In very simple sentences, a student can make his opinion or request known.

> I want to be left alone.
> I want you to be quiet.
> I don't think that is good.
> I don't know about that.
> I have not decided yet.

INTERMEDIATE ASSERTIVE SKILLS.   As a student gains competence in using basic skills, it might be wise to introduce him or her to skills that require a little more social interaction and risk-taking. Again, it is best to apply these skills to specific situations in a student's life.

1. *Agree with It.* If someone criticizes a student or teases him or her in a particularly painful manner, it might be a good idea to take the wind out of the aggressor's sails (so to speak) by simply stating that it may be possible that the aggressor is right. Once you agree with someone, or seem to, there is little reason left for the person to continue the attack. What conflict there is simply disappears or is masked.

> PRINCIPAL: Craig, you are forever doing stupid things. Do you like to
> get caught?
> CRAIG: You may be right. I do stupid things from time to time.

2. *Make a Complaint.* Using this skill, the student makes a criticism about something that is happening. (This is an advanced skill, which is outlined in the following pages.) There is no reference about how to change things. The student simply states his or her opinion, which may or may not involve a feeling. It does involve asking the other for his or her feeling.

> KAREN: [to teacher] You know you gave too much homework last
> night. I had trouble doing all of it inside an hour. What do
> you think about what I just said?

> KATHY: [to teacher] I get angry when you let the boys go to lunch
> first every day. What do you think about this?

3. *Standing Up for One's Rights.* This statement always begins with the words, "It is my right . . . ," and is followed by the infraction or mistake a student feels was made to injure his or her right.

> BEN: It is my right to go home by way of Main Street, and you are
> keeping me from that.
> KERRI: It is my right to have a pencil, and you keep taking mine.

ADVANCED ASSERTIVE SKILLS.   As students begin to cope with acting assertively and as they mature, the more sophisticated assertive skills can be introduced. A student can still use some of the beginning- or intermediate-level skills in conjunction with these. For example, Persistence (Number 2 at the beginning level) could be used with any of the advanced, or even intermediate-level skills.

1. *Nonverbal Assertiveness.* Accompanying the verbal statements are a number of nonverbal assertive actions a student may incorporate. The first involves eye contact. A verbal message of assertiveness becomes intensely more powerful if the student can look the other in the eye. For many students, this is very hard. It is wise to practice direct eye contact over and over again until the student can almost unconsciously employ it. Body posture is also important. One should not direct a verbal assertive message close enough to the other so as to intimidate him or her. A distance of two or three feet away from the other is appropriate, but also allows the student to be in a position of immediacy. The vocal tone of the student should not be so loud that it will appear to be aggressive; nor should it be so soft that it will carry a limp verbal message. Again, it is wise to have the student practice a strong, consistent vocal tone to deliver his or her message. The posture of the student should not include clenched fists, finger-pointing, fidgeting, hands in pockets, or playing with his or her jewelry or pen. Rather, the student should keep his or her hands open, in view, and at his or her side or on a desk. Many assertive guides claim that touching can be a powerful nonverbal assertive skill. However, with students in general, there are problems associated with touching. It is best to counsel students not to touch each other during a verbal exchange. As you read this section on nonverbal behavior, you could get the impression that we are sculpting a student from stone and orchestrating his or her form once. However, as with most behaviors, once a student is taught some of these nonverbal skills, he or she will adapt them to fit his or her personal style. With direction, these nonverbal skills will add strength to the student's overall character.

2. *Negotiate It.* Compromising is a skill to learn. It's a skill in which a person does not surrender rights, but gains results without destroying the integrity of the other. Mutual respect and harmony is the result, for everyone is a winner, and no one loses. The student willing to deal with a conflictual relationship by applying negotiation as the assertive skill will need to prepare several options. These options could be rehearsed with the teacher. Those that are not feasible could be eliminated, and those that work could be enhanced.

The first option is to start by saying "no" to a student's demand, but to offer an alternative to how the request could be carried out.

> MARY: Give me your pen!
> SUE: No. However, if you wait five minutes, I will be done, and then you can borrow it. Or, maybe, you would like to ask Anne to borrow hers, because she is already done.

The second option is to give a choice about when or how something must be done, but not the fact that it must be done.

> BRUCE: I do not care how you get the money or when this week you get it, but I want the quarter you took from my coat.

A third option is to offer and exchange. Here, the student gives up something to gain something.

> MEL: [to Bernadette] Look, you have been borrowing my notebook all week. How about I let you borrow it today, if you let me borrow your pen and pencil case.

A fourth option is to ask the other student for a solution.

> SHIRLEY: Elaine, all week you have been in and out of my desk. How can we come up with a solution to keep you out of my desk for today?

3. *Ask for a Change.* This is the most direct of all assertive responses, since it demands immediate action based on strong feelings. There are three parts to this skill: state a behavior that bothers you; back it up with how you feel about it; and request a specific new behavior to be implemented. Students will need to be coached on this skill. In particular, relating to their feelings will require that they understand how they feel about an issue. To help a student become better aware of his or her feelings, the teacher might use some of the activities in Chapter Four.

> SAM: Every time we go to lunch, Bobby, you run ahead of me to get in line in front. You always push me. This makes me mad. Stop running ahead, and stop pushing me. Wait your turn, like everyone else.

A Final Word about Fight or Flight

Teaching alternative social skills to the typical fight or flight behavior that many students engage in when confronted with a conflictual relationship requires that the teacher become aware of the skills. There is always the question about whether a teacher can teach a skill if he or she does not understand and use it. There are strong advantages for anyone to learn how to behave assertively. For the teacher, any of these assertive skills can be used as part of a repertoire of discipline techniques. For the student, the skills provide a result-oriented, positive, and effective manner to deal with social relations that are demanding, confrontational, or conflictual.

CHAPTER 5 REFERENCES

Aguilera, Donna C., and Janice M. Messick. *Crisis Intervention Theory and Methodology.* St. Louis, MO: C. V. Mosby Co., 1974.

Bolton, Robert. *People Skills: How to Assert Yourself, Listen to Others, and Resolve Conflicts.* Englewood Cliffs, NJ: Prentice Hall, 1979.

Hafen, Bruce Q., and Brenda Peterson. *The Crisis Intervention Handbook.* Englewood Cliffs, NJ: Prentice Hall, 1982.

"Home Team Learning Activities" (pamphlet). Albany, NY: The New York State United Teachers Association, 1986.

Krementz, Jill. *How It Feels When a Parent Dies.* New York: Alfred A. Knopf, 1981.

Morrow, Gertrude. *The Compassionate School: A Practical Guide to Helping Abused and Traumatized Children.* Englewood Cliffs, NJ: Prentice Hall, 1987.

Zembardo, Philip G. *Shyness, What It Is, What to Do About It.* Reading, MA: Addison-Wesley, 1977.

INDEX

204   INDEX